The
PERSONALITY
Workbook

Sue Stockdale and Clive Steeper

First published in Great Britain in 2013 by Hodder & Stoughton. An Hachette UK company.

First published in US in 2013 by The McGraw-Hill Companies, Inc.

This edition published 2013

Copyright © Sue Stockdale and Clive Steeper 2013

The right of Sue Stockdale and Clive Steeper to be identified as the Authors of the Work has been asserted by them in accordance with the Copyright, Designs and Patents Act 1988.

Database right Hodder Education (makers)

The *Teach Yourself* name is a registered trademark of Hachette UK.

British Library Cataloguing in Publication Data: a catalogue record for this title is available from the British Library.

Library of Congress Catalog Card Number: on file.

10 9 8 7 6 5 4 3 2 1

The publisher has used its best endeavours to ensure that any website addresses referred to in this book are correct and active at the time of going to press. However, the publisher and the author have no responsibility for the websites and can make no guarantee that a site will remain live or that the content will remain relevant, decent or appropriate.

The publisher has made every effort to mark as such all words which it believes to be trademarks. The publisher should also like to make it clear that the presence of a word in the book, whether marked or unmarked, in no way affects its legal status as a trademark.

Every reasonable effort has been made by the publisher to trace the copyright holders of material in this book. Any errors or omissions should be notified in writing to the publisher, who will endeavour to rectify the situation for any reprints and future editions.

Cover image © Form Advertising/Alamy

Typeset by Cenveo® Publisher Services.

Printed and bound by CPI Group (UK) Ltd, Croydon, CR0 4YY

Hodder & Stoughton policy is to use papers that are natural, renewable and recyclable products and made from wood grown in sustainable forests. The logging and manufacturing processes are expected to conform to the environmental regulations of the country of origin.

Hodder & Stoughton Ltd

338 Euston Road

London NW1 3BH

www.hodder.co.uk

Acknowledgements

Thanks to everyone who helped us with inspiration, ideas and support during the process of writing this book, in particular Adrian Rees, Geoff Trickey, Bethan Greenall, Tony Nutley, Charlotte Howard, Sherry Harsch-Porter, Sharon Birkman Fink, Dr Paul Brown and our colleagues at the Association for Coaching.

Thanks also to all those who have influenced us over the years. To Sam, Alex, Jenna and Connor: may your personalities be an inspiration to others.

Meet the authors

Sue Stockdale helps leaders globally to achieve improved performance. As an executive coach, Sue brings a powerful combination of psychological insight and business acumen to her work, enabling clients to reflect on aspects of their personality that influence their success. Sue has an MBA in Entrepreneurship and a Masters degree in Quality Management.

Sue has demonstrated the principles in this book through her many achievements, which include being the first British woman to ski to the North Pole and representing Scotland in athletics. She is author of several books on change, leadership and motivation.

Clive Steeper is an executive coach, performance consultant and facilitator, working globally with many organizations ranging from international corporations to fast-growth businesses. A business leader for more 25 years, Clive has had several roles as Managing Director in the UK, USA and Asia. Central to his success has been his ability to help individuals understand how performance is as much about mindset as it is about activity.

Having excelled in motorsport, as an engineer and team manager, today he enjoys competing in a UK championship for sports prototypes. Clive is also co-author, with Sue, of *Cope with Change at Work* (2012).

Contents

Introduction

- ▶ *Do you ever wonder why some people seem more difficult to get on with than others?*
- ▶ *Would you like to achieve more than you currently do but do not feel sure how to begin?*
- ▶ *Have there been times in your life when you've asked yourself some big questions or faced a big challenge?*
- ▶ *Have you ever wondered why things have not worked out as expected in your life so far?*

If you answered yes to one or more of these questions, this book can help you.

To discover answers, you must be prepared to look inside yourself to understand more about your personality and what makes you tick. Once you have that knowledge, you can use it to help you set and achieve goals more effectively and get on with others more easily. You can develop new ways of operating and make different choices in order to get what you want.

Personality is a fascinating subject and there is much to observe and learn about others when we employ all our senses. No two people are the same and it is our ability to value and adapt to that diversity that is important in today's world.

The writing of this book has been an enjoyable and reflective process and, at the outset, we had to look at our own personalities and how we worked together. As a result, we were reminded of how we have changed over time and have learned to adapt to the behaviour of others.

→ How to use this workbook

This book has been designed as a pragmatic tool and not as an in-depth academic study or a review of personality or psychometric assessment tools. The chapters are filled with practical exercises that offer you the opportunity to explore your understanding of yourself and to consider yourself from perspectives you might not have considered before.

While there may well be some uncomfortable moments of self-realization for you, you will find that there will be even more 'light bulb' moments where you discover that there are changes you can make which will improve your performance and enable you to reach your goals. Equally, as you consider the personalities of people you know or work with, this workbook will offer you insights that will further your understanding and appreciation of others and enable you to celebrate and embrace the differences we all bring to the rich tapestry of human culture.

It is often said that we continue to learn throughout our lives. Perhaps also we continue to remember and realize that there is much that we can do yet don't do. We hope this book gives you similar insights and tools to adapt your personality to achieve your goals.

Exercise A

Write down your responses to the questions below.

→ What would you like to achieve as a result of reading this book?

_____

_____

_____

_____

→ How will you know you have achieved your outcome? What will be different?

_____

_____

_____

_____

_____

WORKBOOK OVERVIEW

This book will take you on a journey of self-discovery. It begins with a discussion of what personality is, and then helps you to identify how to adapt your personality in order to be able to set and achieve goals, monitor progress and manage your performance, now and in the future. Each chapter focuses on a different topic area, and begins with four related questions, which are then discussed in more detail.

To use this book, you will need something to write with, and a willingness to participate in and learn from the exercises throughout each chapter. The 12 chapters cover six main themes, outlined below. The tools and techniques explained will provide you with a simple and powerful way to be yourself at your best, in work and in life.

What is personality?

Chapters 1, 2 and 3 explain how temperament and character define our personality. They will also help you become aware of the variety of personality assessments on the market, what their differences are and how to use them effectively.

Assessing where you are

Chapters 4 and 5 discuss the 'five dimensions of personality' as identified by researchers worldwide as the basis for the structure of personality. These chapters also highlight the links between your personality traits and how you tend to go about setting and achieving goals.

Setting goals

Chapters 6 and 7 are about setting goals, using the knowledge from the previous two chapters. In Chapter 6 you will learn how to set goals that will motivate you, and Chapter 7 explains how they can be affected by the wider external environment.

Taking practical steps to improve

Chapter 8 helps you learn how to work with people who have different personality traits from yours. Chapter 9 allows you to focus on your own inner performance, examining the unconscious patterns of behaviour and mindset that influence results.

Monitoring your progress

Chapters 10 and 11 guide you through maintaining progress towards your goals. They will help you understand how your personality is likely to impact on how you select measures to motivate and inform you about how you are doing, and the pace at which you prefer to progress.

The future

Chapter 12 will help you sustain action and learning from the exercises in this workbook, in order to achieve different results in the future.

LEARNING METHODOLOGY

This workbook is written so that you can progress through a series of questions, activities and exercises, then apply the learning immediately to achieve results. Do the exercises a few at a time, to allow for reflection, action and observations. You'll be able to use the knowledge you gain about your personality to help you make positive change in your life, identify goals and work out how to reach them.

A key component of the learning in this workbook is that you write down your answers in the book itself. This is not just to provide a clear record of your responses but also, more importantly, to help you begin the commitment to learning and development and to make adjustments to your personality and understanding of others.

It's all too easy to think about an answer and say, 'Right, I've got that,' when you may not have. Committing the answers to text is psychologically more persuasive to your inner self as it represents a contract between your conscious and subconscious mind. Reading the answers aloud can also provide a useful 'honesty' check of whether what you wrote is what you meant. Sometimes, when we listen to what we've written, we may wince or hear our inner self saying, 'That doesn't seem right.' We should listen and take note of those situations because, if we don't retain our personal integrity, any adjustments we try to make to our personality are in danger of being disingenuous.

It is important to keep in mind that this workbook is for you – and as such there are no right or wrong answers to the questions asked about you. The answers represent your thinking at the time of writing and are open for change by you. The journey through this workbook may well bring about changes in how you view yourself and others and how you might want to be in the future. Therefore consider any sense of change with an open mind. Before any change or committing to the answers you write, there is always the opportunity to reflect.

Whether you complete the exercises in this book in the order given or choose your own order of completion, we highly recommend that you date each written entry. Recording a date next to the completed exercises will enable you to track your progress, and when you review your entries later as part of your continuous personal development, you will be better able to assess the progress you made.

Most of the exercises in this workbook take the form of a series of questions relating to the section you have just read. They give you the opportunity to reflect on their relevance and appropriateness to you. Depending on your goals and ability, as well as your willingness to stretch your comfort zones, you may find it challenging to go for the level of change you might aspire to. Therefore use this workbook to really stretch yourself to discover how much you can develop your personality, as well as to appreciate and work with people who have different personality characteristics from you.

WHAT IS PERSONALITY?

Within the context of this workbook it is important to define what is meant by personality. According to the dictionary, it is the *combination of characteristics or qualities that form an individual's distinctive character.*

In general, there is a recognizable regularity to an individual's behaviour. We expect people to act in the same or similar ways in a variety of situations. Personality influences how we respond to our environment, but also predisposes us to act in certain ways. It is also wider than just what we do. Our personality can be seen in how we think, feel, respond and relate to others.

Exercise B

1   Write down in a few words how you think your best friend would describe your personality.

_____

_____

2   How do you think your manager at work would describe your personality?

_____

_____

3   Notice if there are any similarities or differences between these two descriptions and consider why that might be.

_____

_____

Take the example of two business partners, John and Mary, who run a small business together. Mary enjoys coming up with innovative ways of marketing their products, while John is quick to spot the flaw in any new idea or concept, which Mary has found frustrating. When they go to a networking meeting, however, John would rather be anywhere else, and loathes having to make 'small talk' with complete strangers.

Mary, on the other hand, loves meeting new people. Whereas John will tend to hide by the buffet or get out his phone and look engrossed in his latest email message, Mary will be smiling and chatty. She generally comes away from networking events with a handful of business cards and the intention to follow up with her new acquaintances and find out more about what they do.

Their different personality traits cause them to behave in contrasting ways. It could seem like a recipe for disaster, but they have learned over the years to value one another's differences and play to their strengths in order to make their business succeed and to have a harmonious working environment. John helped them avoid costly mistakes by spotting errors in the packaging design before it went to print, and Mary has managed to maintain good working relationships with their key suppliers and clients with her charm and friendliness. Together, their different personalities combine to make a strong team.

It does not matter what the situation is but, through understanding yourself and how your personality impacts on others and what you want to achieve, it can help you make small changes that can deliver big results.

PERSONALITY, PERCEPTION AND PERFORMANCE

Personality is a subject that is taking centre stage these days, and it is seen as an important aspect of our effectiveness. You only have to turn on the TV or read a newspaper to observe the different types of personalities in the public eye. Some people are chatty, gregarious and lively, while others appear to be reticent, shy and less comfortable with being the focus of attention. What makes the difference is their personality – and many have used their personality to help them achieve success.

Personality has been the subject of study since ancient times, when philosophers and physicians attempted to categorize and define different personality types (see the section on the historical context in Chapter 1). Then as now, and whether we realize it or not, we make judgements about other people's personalities every day, and we use that information in our interactions with them. In exactly the same way, other people are making judgements about us, so this process impacts on our lives at work and at home.

There are two axes of perception vs. self-perception: the first is how we perceive others and how others perceive us, and the second is how we perceive ourselves and how others perceive themselves. These two axes are very influential in terms of the link between personality and performance. If we are open, friendly and seem trustworthy, we are likely to achieve more than if we are quiet, straight-faced and do not acknowledge others.

Similarly, if people respond to us favourably, then our confidence and therefore our performance are likely to be better. Now this might seem obvious, yet how often does this not happen? Could it be because we were in the 'wrong mood', we misunderstood what was said (or written) or we simply saw someone's body language and made a quick judgement (or used our intuition) and said, 'What's the point? They are not really interested.' Understanding and being in control of our personality can be one of our most powerful influencing tools.

You may be wondering how it is possible to change your personality, so it will surprise you to know that you can, and that you are probably already doing so to get the results you want. Although we all have a core personality profile that we develop in our early years, it is more than possible for most of us to modify our personality and therefore our behaviour and even our habits!

By understanding more about your personality, you can develop new and even more effective ways of behaving that will help you get different results.

Exercise C

As you begin the journey into this book to discover more about personality, in particular your own, here is an exercise to help you begin to capture aspects of your character through a few questions.

→ How would you describe your personality?

_____

_____

_____

_____

2 → Review the words you wrote down in the previous exercise about how you think others describe your personality.

_____

_____

_____

_____

3 → What can you do to find out how others actually describe you?

_____

_____

_____

_____

4 → On a scale of 1 to 10, where 1 is low and 10 is high, circle a number below to indicate how much you want to find out how others view you.

1   2   3   4   5   6   7   8   9   10

5 → What aspects of your personality would you like to change?

_____

_____

_____

_____

6 → What would be the benefits of making the personality changes you described?

_____

_____

_____

_____

7 → Circle a number below to indicate how committed you are to making these personality changes happen, where 1 is low commitment and 10 is high.

1   2   3   4   5   6   7   8   9   10

What I have learned

REFLECTIONS

What are my thoughts, feelings and insights on what I have read so far?

YOUR JOURNEY

Use the table below to summarize any actions you identify as a result of reading this introduction.

Chapter	Actions
Introduction	

Where to next?

Now that you understand how this workbook has been designed and written, it is time to begin the journey of understanding personality. One activity that will be constant throughout this book is the concept of keeping a reflective journal. Take a few moments at the end of each chapter to record your thoughts and feelings about what you have just read and how it makes you feel. Then, as you progress through the book, you will be able to monitor how each stage of the journey has an impact on your learning and future actions.

Be curious and enjoy the challenges and knowledge that lie beneath the exploration into personality!

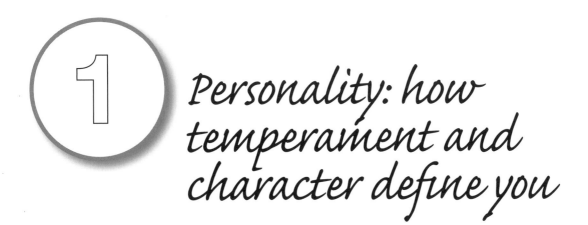

Personality: how temperament and character define you

- ▶ *Do you know how the concept of personality was developed?*
- ▶ *How would you describe your temperament?*
- ▶ *To what degree has your personality changed over the years?*
- ▶ *What situations or people cause you to adapt your personality?*

In this chapter you'll learn how temperament and character shape who we are and find out more about how personality develops. You'll discover how research into personality throughout the centuries has furthered our knowledge of the subject. While this book is not intended to be an academic study of personality, this chapter looks at the early history of inquiry into the subject as it forms the foundation of modern-day work and so many of the tools and models you may come across.

You'll also learn how our senses stimulate our personality and cause us to behave in different ways. The important message is that we can change our personality. Reflect on how you may do this already, recognizing that while it may not always be easy, it is possible.

→ Personality and the historical context

Exactly when the study of personality began is not certain. Both the ancient Egyptians and Greek physicians explored what we now call personality. The Greek physician Hippocrates postulated that there were four bodily fluids, called 'humours'. These were blood (red), yellow bile, black bile and phlegm (blue). These four humours affected human personality, moods, emotions, traits and behaviours, giving rise to four temperaments:

▶ sanguine – pleasure-seeking and sociable

▶ choleric – ambitious and leader-like

▶ melancholic – introverted and thoughtful

▶ phlegmatic – relaxed and quiet.

Exercise 1.1

THE FOUR TEMPERAMENTS

Match the four emotion icons below to the four temperaments:

Answer: Clockwise from top left – phlegmatic, choleric, melancholic and sanguine

Exercise 1.2

WHAT'S YOUR TEMPERAMENT?

Think about which of the emotion icons in the previous exercise most typically represents your face when you are performing the actions below. Have fun sketching the emotion icon in the box opposite each action, or simply write in the temperament.

Speaking to others	
Listening to others	
Working	

Notice how your temperament may be different depending on what you are doing, for example being asked to sketch rather than write your answer.

THE FOUR ELEMENTS AND PERSONALITY

A Greek pre-Socratic philosopher, Empedocles, is regarded as being the originator of the cosmogenic theory of the four classical elements, or 'roots' – earth, water, air and fire. Galen (AD 131–200), an important early writer on the subject of medicine, used this theory of the four elements in his search for physiological reasons for different behaviour in humans. He developed the first typology of temperament in his dissertation *De temperamentis*, in which he mapped these behaviours to a matrix of hot/cold and dry/wet taken from the four elements.

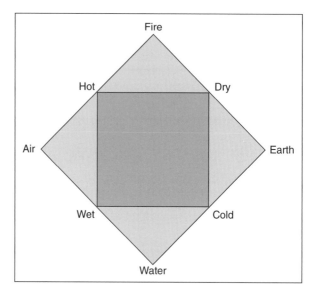

Galen's matrix of the elements

According to Galen, these elements were used by Hippocrates in describing the human body in association with the four humours: yellow bile (fire), black bile (earth), blood (air) and phlegm (water). Aristotle, another famous ancient Greek, proposed a fifth element, aether, which he viewed as a highly concentrated pure essence (quintessence). He thought that earth, water, air and fire were 'of the world' and corruptible, while the stars must be made from a different, unchangeable, heavenly substance.

•Earth	Cold and dry	Today this is regarded as a solid.
•Water	Cold and wet	Today this is regarded as a liquid.
•Air	Hot and wet	Today this is regarded as a gas.
•Fire	Hot and dry	Today this is regarded as heat.
Aether	Considered as the divine substance which constitutes the heavenly spheres and bodies (stars and planets)	

Exercise 1.3

WHAT'S YOUR QUINTESSENCE?

Often we can sum up the essence (quintessence) of an individual in just a few words, for example, 'John helps others to flourish by enabling them to see the best in themselves.'

Think about the quintessence of your personality. What words spring to mind? Write them here.

_____

_____

_____

_____

It was believed that each of the four earthly elements have their natural place and therefore gravitate towards it, rather like the way we have our natural personality that we can adapt, but a tendency to revert back if new habits are not developed.

▶ The earthly element tends towards the centre of the universe.

▶ Water tends towards being a sphere surrounding the centre.

▶ Air tends towards a sphere surrounding the water sphere.

▶ Fire tends towards the lunar sphere (i.e. where the moon orbits).

It was also thought that, when elements are moved out of their natural place, their natural tendency is to go back to their original position. This is 'natural motion' – when, for example, earthy bodies sink in water while air bubbles rise; and when, in air, rain falls and flame rises.

Links for the concept of these five elements can be found in many philosophies, including Hinduism, Buddhism and the cultures of China and Japan. In Hinduism, the four 'roots' elements describe 'matter' and the fifth element describes that which is beyond the material world. With Buddhism, the four 'root' elements are substances to which two others are sometimes added, and regarded as sensory experience.

All these teachings seem to conclude that we all have our natural way of being – which relates to, and is stimulated by, other elements around us. What is your natural way of being?

Exercise 1.4

THE FOUR TEMPERAMENTS

The influence and legacy of these philosophers and physicians of ancient times is immense and worthy of consideration in terms of our own temperament. Take a few minutes to do this exercise by filling in the table below.

→ Think of a situation where you have successfully used each of the four temperament elements in your behaviour.

→ Indicate the order of preference in which you naturally exhibit the four temperaments.

Temperament	Successful situation	Natural preference (1–4)
Choleric (ambitious and leader-like)		
Melancholic (introverted and thoughtful)		
Phlegmatic (relaxed and quiet)		
Sanguine (pleasure-seeking and sociable)		

PERSONALITY STIMULUS

Our personality rarely remains absolutely consistent for long. Why is that? In part it is because at least one of our five primary senses – vision, hearing, touch, taste and smell – will have noticed a change. Since the primary role of our brain is to protect itself, it is continually using the five primary senses to scan the environment for threats.

As a by-product of this information, our personality may be adjusted. The degree to which our personality changes is a mixture of the interpreted risk that has been sensed and the familiarity (training) we have in controlling ourselves. Another factor will be the situation we are in; for example, some people need silence when studying whereas others like music in the background. Two elements that will influence the level of protection we want is our propensity for risk and our mental toughness, which we will cover in more detail in Chapter 8.

Exercise 1.5

FEARS AND MOTIVATIONS

Think about the environment in which you most want to change your personality and list in the table below the five things you fear most and the five things that motivate you most to make that change.

Fears	Motivations
1	1
2	2
3	3
4	4
5	5

Along with the brain's fundamental need to protect itself there is a natural level for us to be 'energized' and have things that we can put our energies into. This level varies from person to person and can be derived from many of the personality assessment tools that identify character types, personality traits and behaviours.

WHERE DOES YOUR ENERGY COME FROM?

Typically, we receive our energies (stimulus) either from the external world or from within ourselves (internal) and we put our energies into either people or task-related actions. Examples of some actions are listed in the table below.

→ Read through the list and consider what the stimulus is for doing them.

Activity	External or internal stimulus?
Agreeing to help out at a local school event with other parents	
Crewing on a friend's yacht	
Planning a dinner party and thinking of menu ideas	
Painting a picture	
Enjoying beautiful scenery while walking the dog	
Organizing your CD collection into alphabetical order	

→ Now we can begin to explore personality stimulus. Use the following table to write down examples of where you prefer to get your energy (stimulus) from, both externally and internally.

Externally (e.g. outdoors, being active, with others)		Internally (e.g. reflective activities, mental stimulation)	
Daily life (e.g. at work)	Personal life (e.g. at home or in hobby/interest)	Daily life (e.g. at work)	Personal life (e.g. at home or in hobby/interest)

→ What do you prefer to put your energy into?

People (e.g. helping others, family, friends)		Tasks (e.g. directing, controlling, initiating)	
Daily life (e.g. at work)	Personal life (e.g. at home or in hobby/interest)	Daily life (e.g. at work)	Personal life (e.g. at home or in hobby/interest)

→ Now revisit your fears and motivations from Exercise 1.5 and tick the boxes below according to whether they are externally or internally energized and people- or task-orientated.

Fears				
Description	Stimulus		Orientation	
	External	Internal	People	Task

Motivations				
Description	Stimulus		Orientation	
	External	Internal	People	Task

→ Using your answers in the tables above, enter your preference into the EIPT model below for (i) where you take your energy (stimulus) from and (ii) where you prefer to put your energies.

External	People
Internal	Task

This knowledge will help you navigate through other chapters in this book where this table will be referenced.

Case study

Sherry loved making things happen and, as a team leader at work, she thrived on encouraging her team to achieve strict deadlines and deliver tangible outputs. She had the opportunity to take the Myers-Briggs Type Indicator (MBTI®) assessment as part of a management development programme, and the results helped her to understand more about herself.

Sherry's report identified her as someone with a preference for getting energy from others, which she agreed with: she hated to be given work that she had to tackle on her own. (Once, when she broke her ankle and could not drive, she had found the two weeks working from home a challenge.) The report also highlighted her preference for using her senses and logic to make decisions.

One day she met a colleague to discuss a project. As they chatted, Sherry realized that they were each concerned about different aspects of the project. Sherry always picked up on spelling errors and inconsistencies in documents and was concerned to make sure they had a plan, whereas her colleague was more interested in broad concepts and the possibilities for the future of the business if their proposal was agreed. Her colleague was also very quiet and enjoyed meetings with just the two of them rather than the entire project team.

Sherry thought back to her MBTI preferences and acknowledged that she and her colleague were energized by different aspects of the work. In order for them to work well together, Sherry decided that, rather than getting annoyed about the differences, she needed to embrace and value them.

PERSONALITY IMPACT

From what has been said already, it is clear that the concepts of personality, perception and performance are intertwined. From this it can be seen that personality affects us both passively, by what happens to us when others communicate to us, as well as dynamically by the mood and mindset we adopt.

In other words, the ability to adapt how we react to what happens around us is controlled by our brain. With the advancement of neuroscience, scientists now confirm that the complex combination of chemicals in our brain (over 100) controls us to a greater degree than we ever imagined. The emotional system is part of that concoction and both regulates and is regulated by the brain. It consists of eight basic emotions:

- ▶ Sadness
- ▶ Shame
- ▶ Disgust
- ▶ Anger

- ▶ Fear
- ▶ Surprise/startle
- ▶ Excitement/joy
- ▶ Love/trust

These emotions can be shown in a spectrum ranging from avoidance behaviour at one end (associated with sadness, shame, disgust, etc.) to attachment behaviour at the other end (associated with joy, love/trust). As human beings have evolved through time, fear is still our default emotion. Fear can be easily triggered, and it requires even more mental effort on our part to override this and choose a different behaviour. These characteristics are innate within us and – combined with what we learn during our lifetime – cause us to behave as we do.

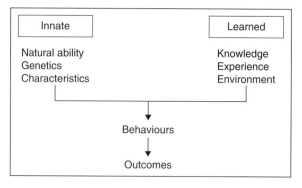

How personality impacts on outcomes

To adapt better to different situations, we can develop a greater range of behaviours by understanding more aspects of our personality.

Exercise 1.7

CONSIDER OUTCOMES

Consider whether you would like to achieve a different outcome in an area of your work or life. Write down below what you would like to be different.

→Work _____

_____

→Life _____

_____

Keep these areas in mind as you read through this book, to help you uncover the aspects of your personality that affect your behaviour which can help or hinder you in achieving the outcome you want.

YOUR CHARACTER TODAY

Your personality makes you unique and different from all other humans. As we have seen, our personality is a combination of innate traits – those we are born with – and the habits we develop over time, based on the environment we have experienced and the knowledge we have gained during our lifetime.

How our personality and character develop is a function of choices, some conscious and some unconscious. We use the unconscious choices when our brain is on its version of autopilot, i.e. the 'program' it uses to respond quickly to threats. In early times humans had to run from animals and danger; now these so-called dangers tend to be different, but our responses are often the same as ever.

For example, if your friends laughed at you when you danced as a child, it's likely that you have developed a response over time of 'If I dance, people will laugh at me,' which now limits your choice of behaviour when you hear energetic music. If you had been encouraged to dance as a child, it's likely that you would be less self-conscious about dancing as an adult.

As you explore your personality through this workbook, consider the choices you made that define you today and what areas you may wish to change in future so that your choices make a positive difference to your personality.

Case study

Caroline was a quiet, sensitive young woman who rarely made her views known in a group setting, as she was fearful of being challenged or questioned. She felt frustrated because she had recently been passed over for promotion in favour of a more confident, more vociferous colleague. When Caroline asked her manager for feedback, she was told that she needed to be more influential and confident, as the selection panel had felt she did not make an impact. At that moment Caroline decided she needed to change.

That evening, Caroline had a long chat with her grandmother whom she regarded as a wise lady. Caroline recalled that as a child she had often felt awkward when her father questioned her on a subject they were discussing around the dinner table, and her brothers had laughed at her because she could not always come up with an answer. This had put her off speaking up in a group and made her feel self-conscious.

Her grandmother listened intently. 'I'm not sure if you know this,' she said, 'but your father really wanted you to develop an inquiring mind and not just accept what you were told by others. His intention was to encourage you to think for yourself.'

Caroline had never realized this before. The more she talked with her grandmother, the more she understood that she did think for herself but felt challenged by sharing her thoughts with another person. However, just because her brothers had laughed at her did not mean that everyone would have the same reaction.

As they talked, Caroline's grandmother asked her, 'What exactly are you going to change?' and, more importantly, 'How much do you really want to change?' and pointed out that she should be prepared to go through feeling uncomfortable for a while.

Caroline thought about this second question for a few moments. Her grandmother said, 'Given that change can be difficult and stressful, it's important that you review your reasons for change and are clear that it really means something to you, and that you are changing for yourself, not for someone else. From what you've told me, maybe you should start off by sharing your views with someone you think is likely to be encouraging and supportive, before you tackle those who may challenge you.'

Later, as Caroline drove home, she realized that she could change her behaviour, and she was determined to give it a try because it would benefit all aspects of her life.

Whatever aspect of your personality you decide to change, you only have to decide to do it, and then keep practising.

Exercise 1.8

WHAT WOULD YOU LIKE TO CHANGE?

Review the outcomes that you wrote down from Exercise 1.7. These were things that you would like to be different in your life or work.

Now take a minute – no more – to complete the following exercise.

→ I would like to change the _____ part of my personality, which will help me to achieve a different outcome in my work/life (as described above)

_____

→ One small step that will help me to do this is

_____

→ I intend to start this action by

_____

What I have learned

REFLECTION

Take a few moments to record your thoughts, feelings and insights about what you have read so far.

YOUR JOURNEY

Summarize any actions you have identified as a result of reading this chapter.

Chapter	Actions
Introduction	
What is personality? 1 Personality: how temperament and character define you	

Where to next?

As the journey into understanding personality develops, the next chapter will take you into the world of personality assessments, which are used by many organizations for job recruitment as well as personal development. It will explain more about some of the well-known types of personality assessments, including the Myers-Briggs Type Indicator (MBTI), 16PF, OPQ and DISC, as well as defining the difference between types and traits. This should enable you to be better informed should you then wish to take any of these assessments after reading this workbook.

2 Personality assessment tools and tests

- ▶ What are the different types of personality assessment tools?
- ▶ Have you ever completed a personality assessment?
- ▶ If you did, what did you learn from it?
- ▶ What is the purpose of personality assessment tools?

Personality assessments may be carried out using any of a broad range of evaluation tools that measure a person's knowledge, abilities or personality or a combination of any of these three elements. Personality assessments originate from the branch of psychology that deals with the design, administration and interpretation of quantitative tests for the measurement of psychological variables such as intelligence, aptitude and personality traits.

In this chapter you will learn more about the purpose of personality assessment tools and psychometric tests, and identify some of the more popular tools and how they are used in a work context. They are most commonly used for job selection processes and, increasingly, to help with personal development.

'The illiterate of the 21st century will not be those who cannot read and write, but those who cannot learn, unlearn and relearn.'

Alvin Toffler, author (b. 1928)

→ What are personality assessments?

The roots of personality assessments, or 'psychometrics' as they are sometimes known, are in the related field of psychophysics (commonly defined as the quantitative branch of the study of perception, examining the relations between observed stimuli and responses and the reasons for those relations). Much early theoretical and applied work was around trying to measure intelligence.

As psychometric theory developed, people began to apply it to the measurement of personality, particularly attitudes and beliefs, as well as to health-related fields and academic achievement. Hundreds of different tests are available, and some are more statistically reliable and easier to complete than others. Measurement of these unobservable aspects of personality can be difficult and as such is open to challenge.

Critics have expressed concerns that the measurements can easily be misused. However, psychometric professionals counter the critics by pointing out that only those who are qualified should carry out the measurements and interpretation of assessments.

The British Psychological Society defines a psychometric test as 'any procedure on the basis of which inferences are made concerning a person's capacity, propensity or liability to act, react, experience, or to structure or order thought or behaviour in particular ways'.

Personality testing used to be done and administered only through assessment centres or face-to-face meetings. However, with the advent of the Internet, secure online assessments are becoming popular as part of the initial assessment process. Feedback is usually provided by computer-generated reports and delivered in face-to-face meetings, where a fuller, two-way feedback dialogue can be conducted with the benefit of evaluating body language and the human chemistry of 'being present physically'. Often where feedback is conducted over the telephone, there can be a greater likelihood of misunderstanding.

→ What do these tests measure?

Over the last few decades, psychological or psychometric tests have been used in an ever-increasing range of applications to assess ability, personality, behaviour and interests, ranging from job interviews, military and government roles to assessing students in education, prison offenders and those with mental health issues.

There are two broad types of psychological test:

- ▶ **tests of ability, aptitude or attainment,** commonly referred to as measures of maximum performance
- ▶ **tests to assess personal qualities,** which are referred to as measures of typical performance. These qualities include values, beliefs, personality, social interests, interpersonal skills, motivation, drive, risk propensity, mental toughness and developmental and personal needs.

Within these two categories are a number of different types of test and assessment, including:

- ▶ **aptitude tests,** which measure how people differ in their ability to perform or carry out different tasks
- ▶ **behaviour/interest tests,** which measure how people vary in their motivation, the direction and strength of their interests, plus their values and opinions
- ▶ **personality assessments,** which measure how people differ in their style or manner of doing things, as well as the way they interact with their environment and other people (personality).

Other terms you may come across for these three categories of tests are ability tests, interest inventories and personality questionnaires.

ABILITY OR APTITUDE TEST

This measures how well a person can perform a function or functions, how much they know about the function or activity, and occasionally what their potential is. Intellectual abilities such as verbal fluency or numerical reasoning may also be tested, along with more role- or function-specific practical tests. These tests are usually timed and require either 'yes or no', 'right or wrong' or 'good or bad' answers. Popular examples of ability tests are verbal reasoning and numerical and critical thinking appraisal.

Exercise 2.1

Think about a situation at work when it would be useful to use an ability test and write it down in the space below.

_____

BEHAVIOUR/INTEREST INVENTORY

This is used to assess and explore a person's preferred working style, their likes and dislikes, plus their attitudes to external influences, for example scientific or artistic activities. The assessments have no right or wrong answers as they are self-reporting. They are not usually timed.

Exercise 2.2

Think about a team situation at work when it would be useful to use a behaviour inventory. Write it down in the space below.

_____

PERSONALITY ASSESSMENT

This measures your preferred or typical way of being, i.e. it assesses and measures your underlying traits and characteristics. The style of the questionnaires is self-reporting so there are no right or wrong answers. They are not usually timed, but individuals are encouraged to answer quickly, i.e. go with their first thought rather than dwell and become confused. It is also recommended that the assessments be completed in one sitting. The majority of personality questionnaires that are used in work contexts, rather than clinically, are categorized as either type- or trait-based.

Exercise 2.3

Think about a recruitment situation at work when it would be useful to use a personality assessment. Write it down in the space below.

_____

TYPE INDICATORS

The type indicators originate from ancient times, when they were described as the four temperaments (see Chapter 1), and were significantly enhanced by Carl Jung's work in recent times where he established the difference between extravert and introvert personality types. The two best-known approaches are the Myers-Briggs Type Indicator® and DiSC®.

Myers-Briggs

Isabel Myers and Katharine Briggs built on Jung's work and constructed the Myers-Briggs Type Indicator (MBTI), which remains one of the most well-known occupational psychometric instruments. The MBTI assesses an individual's preferences in relation to four attributes, as shown in the table below.

MBTI parameters	
Extraversion	Introversion
Sensing	Intuition
Thinking	Feeling
Judging	Perceiving

DiSC

Another highly popular type-based assessment tool was initiated in the 1920s through theoretical work led by William Moulton Marston and has become known as DiSC® (standing for dominance, influence, steadiness and conscientiousness). He believed that everyone exhibits these four characteristics but in varying amounts.

DiSC® evolved through three main stages, led firstly by Marston then built upon by Walter Clarke, who created an assessment personality profile test using Marston's theories, along with John Cleaver who further developed the tool.

The third stage involved the creation of 'Self-description' by John Geier within a Personal Profile System® (PPS), where he developed the understanding of 15 basic behaviour patterns.

DiSC parameters	
Dominance	Influence
Steadiness	Conscientiousness

Belbin team types

Another popular type indicator assessment is Meredith Belbin's team types. His work in part originates from work conducted by Henley Business School to develop successful managers who were thought to have potential to become business directors.

Dr Belbin, along with his colleagues, began using the outputs from the exercises that the managers at Henley had done as competing teams. They built on this over a seven-year period by observing many more competing teams taking part in business games; they then recorded and categorized what occurred.

The result was the creation of eight team types, which later became nine types when the role of specialist was added (recognizing their knowledge and ability more than their temperament). The Belbin Inventory scores people on how strongly they express behavioural traits from the following nine different team roles:

- ▶ Plant
- ▶ Resource investigator
- ▶ Co-ordinator
- ▶ Shaper
- ▶ Monitor evaluator
- ▶ Team worker
- ▶ Implementer
- ▶ Completer finisher
- ▶ Specialist

Exercise 2.4

You have now read about three examples of type-based assessments: MBTI, DiSC and Belbin team roles. Tick any of the other popular type- and trait-based assessments that you have either heard about or completed yourself, listed here.

Insights Discovery	Risk Type Compass	MTQ48
16PF	Birkman	OPQ32
4G	Thomas International	McQuaig
Enneagram	Strengths Finder	Hogan

If you completed any of these assessments yourself, what did you learn as a result?

_____

_____

_____

TRAIT-BASED ASSESSMENTS

Trait indicators are more quantitative than type indicators and aim to measure a number of dimensions that constitute someone's personality. There are a number of popular dimension sets (or scales) used as the basis of psychometric assessments, the most popular of which are:

▶ Raymond Cattell = 16 dimensions

▶ Hans Eysenck = 21 dimensions

▶ Saville & Holdsworth = 32 dimensions.

The numbers in some of the assessment descriptions, such as OPQ32 and 16PF, indicate dimensions. Both type- and trait-based assessments are described in more detail in Chapter 3.

→ The 'Big Five' personality dimensions

The 'Big Five' personality dimensions are often referred to as OCEAN. The five dimensions are extraversion, neuroticism, conscientiousness, agreeableness and openness to experience (see Chapter 4 for more details).

16PF

The 16 Personality Factors Questionnaire (16PF) was created by Raymond Cattell in the 1940s and has been updated five times. The 16PF fifth edition has 185 multiple-choice questions about your regular behaviour, interests and opinions. Since words can be misunderstood or misinterpreted, the factors are also given an 'alpha' (letter) code, as shown in the table below.

16PF (Cattell's 16 Personality Factors)			
Warmth (A)	Impulsivity (F)	Scepticism (L)	Openness to change (Q1)
Intelligence (B)	Conformity (G)	Imagination (M)	Self-reliance (Q2)
Emotional stability (C)	Boldness (H)	Privateness (N)	Perfectionism (Q3)
Dominance (E)	Sensitivity (I)	Insecurity (O)	Irritability (Q4)

EYSENCK PERSONALITY PROFILER

Although somewhat controversial at times, Hans Eysenck was one of the first psychologists to study personality using factor analysis, a statistical method used to describe variability among observed, correlated variables. He created a model of personality known as PEN (which stands for psychoticism, extraversion and neuroticism) and his original work explored personality through two main factors – extraversion and neuroticism.

Neuroticism trait is the tendency to experience negative emotions, and the scale ranges from high – emotional instability and spontaneity – to low – reflection and deliberateness. The extraversion trait covers the tendency to enjoy positive events, such as social occasions, and the scale ranges from high – sociability and stimulation-seeking – to low – social reticence and stimulation avoidance. These two personality dimensions were described in Eysenck's 1947 book *Dimensions of Personality*.

Useful fact

It is common practice in personality psychology to refer to the dimensions by their first letters. For example, extraversion = E and neuroticism = N.

In the late 1970s Eysenck and his wife introduced the third dimension, psychoticism, where the scale ranges from high – aggressiveness and divergent thinking – to low – empathy and caution.

Eysenck Personality Profiler (EPP) (The 21 traits of personality)		
Extraversion	Neuroticism	Psychoticism
Activity	Inferiority	Risk-taking
Sociability	Unhappiness	Impulsivity
Expressiveness	Anxiety	Irresponsibility
Assertiveness	Dependence	Manipulativeness
Ambition	Hypochondria	Sensation-seeking
Dogmatism	Guilt	Tough-mindedness
Aggressiveness	Obsessiveness	Practicality

OPQ32

Saville and Holdsworth's Occupational Personality Questionnaire (OPQ32 model) is based on measuring the preferred behaviour or style of an individual against 32 dimensions (or scales). The results are then distilled into three domains:

▶ feeling (feelings and emotions)

▶ relating (relationships with people)

▶ thinking (thinking style).

A fourth dimension – dynamic – is sometimes also considered. It is composed of dimensions such as achieving, competitive and vigorous. The table below shows the 32 dimensions (or scales) categorized within the three domains.

OPQ32 (Occupational Personality Questionnaire dimensions)		
Feeling	**Relating**	**Thinking**
Relaxed	Persuasive	Data-rational
Worrying	Controlling	Evaluative
Tough-minded	Outspoken	Behavioural
Optimistic	Independent-minded	Conventional
Trusting/critical	Outgoing	Conceptual
Emotional control	Affiliative	Innovative
Vigorous	Socially confident	Variety-seeking
Competitive	Modest	Adaptable
Achieving	Democratic	Forward-thinking
Decisive	Caring	Detail-conscious
		Conscientious
		Rule-following

Originally, OPQ32 was developed with two formats and scales – normative (OPQ32n) and ipsative (OPQ32i), which was forced-choice format. The ipsative version has now been replaced with a forced-choice format version using item response theory, which generates normative scale scores and is referred to as OPQ32r.

An ipsative assessment is based on comparison of a person's current performance or preference with their past performance or preference. For example, when completing an assessment, an individual could be asked to compare two or more desirable options and pick the one that they prefer most. This is sometimes referred to as a 'forced-choice' scale.

→ What do these assessments tell you?

As you can see from the range of dimensions shown for the various type- and trait-based assessments, different dimensions can be used in many ways to describe an individual's personality. By considering the dimensions in relation to yourself, you may well recognize how your temperament is affected by your natural or preferred choice of dimensions. This may give you clues about how your personality operates, i.e. reacts in different situations. Similarly, notice which dimensions you think are 'not you' or you choose not to use in certain situations; they may well have more influence than you originally thought.

All the information on choices and preferences is what lies behind our personality and therefore how we approach each situation we face. Some situations we will deal with naturally, or instinctively, while for others we may develop habits and so make them 'automatic', e.g. thinking styles, feelings and emotions. It is these various approaches that give important clues to those we interact with, directly or indirectly.

An example of indirect interaction is when someone observes you from across a room and creates a first impression of you. That will influence how they react towards you, even though they may have never even spoken to you. Other clues they may glean about your personality are from what you say and how you communicate.

These personality assessment tools can provide information to help a recruiter or employer make a choice between one candidate and another. However, they are not infallible. While many focus on behaviour and show the type of behaviour a person has a natural disposition for, the current work environment can influence the output. For example, if a job demands a level of attention to detail, individuals have the capability to adapt their behaviour to meet that need, even if it may not be their natural preference.

Exercise 2.5

Think of a job or a role you have had in the past where you have had to display aspects of your personality that are not your natural preference. For example, you may have needed to focus on planning ahead when you prefer to leave things to the last minute, or you had to work in a team when you prefer solitary tasks. How easy was it for you to adapt your behaviour? Make notes in the box below.

Not many personality assessments focus on getting to the core motivational level that underlies how people think, relate to others and make decisions, despite the environment in which they operate. So when employers are making a business decision about a candidate or employee, they should ensure that they are determining not only whether a person has the innate capability to do the job in question, but whether the person will truly be motivated and engaged in the task they will be required to undertake.

→ Comparing trait-based assessments

Because of the variety of different trait-based assessments, it can be quite confusing what characteristics each one is highlighting. The following table shows the Five Dimensions of Personality compared to the 16PF and OPQ32 dimensions. Not all the 16PF and OPQ32 dimensions correlate to the Five Dimensions of Personality, but this table will still be helpful to refer back to as you progress through this workbook, particular when you are seeking descriptors and insights to behaviours.

Comparison of trait-based assessments		
Five Dimensions of Personality	16PF	OPQ32
EXTRAVERSION Basic scale: introversion-extraversion	Dominance (E) Impulsivity (F) Boldness (H) Privateness (N)-introversion tendency Openness to change (Q1)-introversion tendency	Optimistic Trusting Emotional control Competitive Achieving Decisive Persuasive Controlling Outspoken Independent-minded Socially confident Modest-introversion tendency Conventional-introversion tendency Innovative Variety-seeking

Five Dimensions of Personality	16PF	OPQ32
NEUROTICISM Basic scale: confident-sensitive	Emotional stability (C) Dominance (E) Impulsivity (F) Conformity (G)-sensitive tendency Insecurity (O))-sensitive tendency Openness to change (Q1)-sensitive tendency Irritability (Q4)	Relaxed Worrying-sensitive tendency Tough-minded Optimistic Persuasive Controlling Outspoken Outgoing Socially confident Modest-sensitive tendency Conventional-sensitive tendency Innovative Variety–seeking
CONSCIENTIOUSNESS Basic scale: unstructured-detail-conscious	Impulsivity (F)-unstructured tendency Conformity (G) Perfectionism (Q3)	Conventional Detail-conscious Conscientious
AGREEABLENESS Basic scale: tough minded-agreeable	Dominance (E) Impulsivity (F) Conformity (G)-agreeable tendency Scepticism (L) Openness to change (Q1) Perfectionism (Q3)-negative responses	Trusting Independent-minded Affiliative-agreeable tendency Caring-agreeable tendency Detail-conscious-agreeable tendency
OPENNESS Basic scale: conforming-creative	Dominance (E) Impulsivity (F)-creative tendency Conformity (G) Boldness (H)-creative tendency Privateness (N) Perfectionism (Q3)	Competitive-creative tendency Achieving-creative tendency Decisive-creative tendency Persuasive-creative tendency Outspoken-creative tendency Outgoing-creative tendency Modest Traditional Innovative-creative tendency

→ Why use personality assessments?

More and more organizations of all sizes are using personality assessments and psychometric testing for a broad range of applications. It is estimated that over 70 per cent of larger companies use personality assessments to gain insights into potential employees as well as existing members of their team. Over the last few decades an increasing number of small businesses have joined the large and medium organizations in using personality assessments.

Employers use these assessments for purposes ranging from recruitment (both internal and external candidates), where the reports will form part of the supporting information about a candidate's suitability, to personal development, talent management, executive coaching and mentoring. These reports provide both the assessor (employer) and the respondent (applicant) with insights into aspects of the respondents' personality such as their behaviour and style.

The benefits to organizations are shown in the following table.

Benefits of using personality assessments	
Purpose	**Benefit**
Validation	Tests are proven and provide a consistent framework and process
Balance	Equality and fairness for all individuals tested
Objectivity	Helps to reduce bias and personal perspective
Trending	Able to predict performance (in various conditions)
Gap analysis	Identification of learning and development needs
Self-improvement	Assessment outputs provide insights and opportunity for individuals to improve themselves

WHAT ARE PSYCHOMETRIC TESTS USED FOR?

There are many different types of personality tests that typically measure skill, ability, intelligence, personality, motivation and interests. The table below offers a list of typical applications at work.

Applications and benefits of testing	
Application	*Benefits*
Recruitment (search and selection)	Test results provide a 'filter' for identifying possible candidates with the appropriate profile. Assessments also provide profiles of candidates that can be used to explore and verify findings.
Careers guidance	For situations such as career development, career change and outplacement, the broad range of psychometric assessment tools can help evaluate suitability and challenges and design the next series of career steps.
Personality profiling	Self-perception and broader perceptions, especially if a '360-degree' assessment is conducted, will help you understand your personality. While personality traits don't generally change, behaviour traits can be modified over time, which may bring about changes to habits.
Leadership and management development	As well as leadership and management style insights, the test can aid understanding of other specific aspects of their role, such as conflict management, mental toughness and risk tolerance.

Team development personality assessments offer powerful insights for individuals within teams to better understand and adjust to working as a more effective team.

GOOD PRACTICE IN PSYCHOMETRIC TESTING

The following three guidelines represent 'good practice' for employers using any form of psychometric test.

1 Don't use them solely for decision making. A personality assessment will only give you one perspective of an individual. Remember to consider other issues such as motivation, interests, sociability, emotional and mental intelligence and existing track record to provide a broader view.

2 Be aware that these are only part of what makes up an individual. When individuals complete assessments, they may misinterpret words or complete the assessment when they are stressed rather than relaxed; even the time of day can bring different results.

3 Use only licensed assessors to conduct assessments and feedback. The reason that it costs time and money to train assessors in the use of a particular assessment tool is to ensure that they can fully understand, administer and interpret the reports correctly.

TIPS FOR TAKING PERSONALITY ASSESSMENTS

If you are going to be taking a personality assessment, you need to know a number of details in advance so that you understand how the information is going to be used and who is going to have access to it. The next exercise will help you find out what you need to know.

Exercise 2.6

You should find out the answers to the following ten questions if you are going to undertake a personality assessment.

- ▶ What is the purpose of me undertaking the assessment?
- ▶ How are the results going to be used?
- ▶ Are the people administering the assessment qualified to do so?
- ▶ How will my results be communicated to me?
- ▶ Who else will have access to the report?
- ▶ How will the information remain confidential?
- ▶ How long is the information stored for?
- ▶ What assurances can you provide that the results are not going to be used for other purposes other than those originally agreed?
- ▶ What type of feedback will I receive?
- ▶ If everyone in our team completes the personality assessment, how will the team results be shared while maintaining my individual privacy?

These questions should help to reassure you that the assessment process is robust and well considered. Note down any other questions that you think are important to ask in the space below.

1 _____

2 _____

3 _____

4 _____

What I have learned

REFLECTIONS

What are my thoughts, feelings and insights on what I have read so far?

```
```

YOUR JOURNEY

Summarize any actions you have identified as a result of reading this chapter.

Chapter	Actions
Introduction	
What is personality? 1 Personality: how temperament and character define you 2 Personality assessment tools and tests	

Where to next?

This chapter has explained what personality assessments are and highlighted some of the more popular assessment tools. It has also helped you understand how assessments are used at work and given you some tips to help you make sure they are used correctly. The next chapter continues to focus on personality assessments and will help you find out how to interpret the information you receive as well as how to use it to generate action and change in the future.

3 How to use personality assessments

- ▶ I received my assessment report. Do I need someone to interpret it for me?
- ▶ What do I do with this information now?
- ▶ Am I normal?
- ▶ How can I verify whether what the report tells me is really correct?
- ▶ Will everyone else interpret my personality assessment in the same way I do?

The more you understand about personality, the better you will be able to judge what motivates you and other people, especially when working in or leading a team. And the more you understand this, the better you will be at knowing how others perceive you and at interpreting their reactions to your own personality and style.

This chapter aims to show you how to interpret the information from a personality assessment and how to verify it by getting other perspectives. Perhaps more importantly, it will also explore the issue of how to use this information in order to generate action for change.

'Personality has the power to open many doors, but character must keep them open.'

Anon.

→ Interpreting personality assessments

Personality assessments are tools that enable you, particularly at work, to:

▶ assess your strengths and examine habits that may be limiting success

▶ create a plan to improve capabilities at work while staying true to your underlying personality traits

▶ step out of your comfort zone and try out different behaviours.

Sometimes you, or others using the report for selection or career development purposes, may misinterpret the results of an assessment at work. It is therefore important to understand how to interpret the information properly so that you know what it is telling you about your personality – and then what to do as a result.

Imagine looking at an Ordnance Survey map of the countryside. You may be able to tell from the map that the area is highly populated and that a river runs through it, but unless you have the ability to identify where you are in relation to where you want to go and can interpret what the map is telling you, as well as its scale, it's not going to help you navigate your way from where you are currently standing to a new location.

In the same way, interpretation of an assessment report is an important part of the assessment process as it helps you understand and use the information to instigate action and change. Most psychological assessments are required to be administered by a certified practitioner, that is, an individual who has undergone training in how to use the tool and how to provide accurate interpretation.

As already described in Chapter 2, personality assessments generally measure two different things: personality traits and personality types.

PERSONALITY TRAITS

A trait is a characteristic pattern of behaviour that is universal to all of us, is relatively stable over time and influences our actions. What differs is the amount of a trait that each of us possesses. For example, we can measure everyone's height and age, but we might describe some people as very tall or really old.

Statisticians generally agree that traits for 68 per cent of the population are in the middle range of a normal distribution curve. It's the personality behaviours that appear out of that norm that we are apt to make judgments about. For example, we might say that someone is very trusting or extremely intelligent.

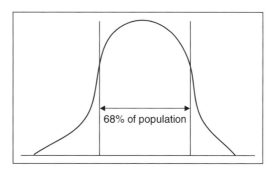

Normal distribution curve for traits

Examples of traits that can be assessed are:

▶ emotional and easily upset vs. calm and stable

▶ suspicious vs. trusting

▶ reserved and unfriendly vs. outgoing and friendly.

Psychologists studying trait theory have identified five basic characteristics that are seen as fundamental to human personality. Most personality assessments are based on these five characteristics, sometimes called the Five Dimensions of Personality or the Big Five. In the next chapter you will be able to complete exercises to help you understand more about these. The subsequent chapters will help you interpret the results and use the data to build on your strengths and change or adapt your less helpful behaviours.

These assessments have generally been developed to address the need to explain personality in contexts such as work as they allow for more accurate comparisons between individuals. For example, they are often used in recruitment and selection, or as part of a coaching programme.

PERSONALITY TYPES

Type-based personality assessments assess an individual's personality by categorizing the person into distinct collections of particular personality traits. These collections then highlight how that person might behave in particular ways in certain situations. Two popular type-based assessments used in the workplace are DiSC and the Myers-Briggs Type Indicator, described in Chapter 2.

These types of assessments are popular because they are easy to understand and can be useful in team-building activities. However, they are generally less psychometrically sound than trait-based assessments because they tend to pigeonhole individuals into particular narrow types. This results in less accurate comparisons between individuals, so they should not be used in activities such as recruitment and selection or for anything that requires accurate differentiation between individuals.

Traits and types compared

Traits	Types
Universal characteristics that we all possess in differing amounts, e.g. trusting	*A collection of traits that are identified together*
Traits cause behaviour. *Trait-based assessments allow for accurate comparison between individuals.*	*Psychological type describes healthy differences between people; it does not explain or measure competence, skills, success factors, excellence, natural ability or psychological problems.*
Scores range across a bell curve normal distribution.	*Psychological type does imply personality preferences.*
Assessment measures 'how much' of a trait an individual possesses.	*They are inborn preferences.*
Trait-based assessments are useful for recruitment and selection.	*Scores categorize people into type groups, e.g. bi-modal – either sensing or intuition (you cannot be both).*
Examples of assessments are Big Five Factors, OPQ, Birkman, 16PF.	*Assessments do not measure 'how much' of the type you have, e.g. if I am more intuitive than you, are my intuitions better?*
	Type-based assessments are useful for team-building activities and coaching. Examples of assessments are DiSC, MBTI, Belbin team roles, Firo-B.

Exercise 3.1

Referring back to Exercise 2.4 and what you learned as a result of taking personality assessments, note down how you applied what you learned in order to make changes for the future.

_____

_____

_____

→ Personality and the Johari Window

One of the things that personality assessments can provide is some insight into facets of our personality that we were unaware of or unwilling to share with others. One model for developing personality awareness, the Johari Window, developed in the 1950s by Joseph Luft and Harry Ingham, explains how feedback and self-disclosure are two activities that can help you discover more about your unknown potential.

The Johari Window is a square diagram divided into four quadrants, called arena, façade, blind spot and unknown, as shown below. Arena is the public arena in which you generally operate and is known to you and others. The areas of the blind spot and façade are characteristics of your personality of which either you or others are unaware. The unknown box is really your unknown potential, and the results of a personality assessment can help you uncover some of these facets, as well as reduce blind spots and façades (things you prefer to keep hidden and private).

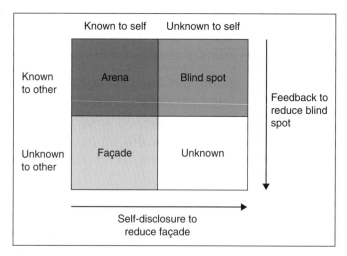

The Johari Window

Exercise 3.2

This exercise enables you to explore the Johari Window in terms of understanding your personality. Use the table below, adapted from aspects of the 16PF questionnaire, to answer the following questions.

Detached	Warm	Emotionally stable	Reactive	Deferential	Dominant
Serious	Lively	Problem solving	Trusting	Vigilant	Sensitive
Unsentimental	Shy	Bold	Expedient	Rule-conscious	Self-assured
Apprehensive	Practical	Imaginative	Conventional	Private	Open
Bright	Traditional	Perfectionist	Self-reliant	Group-focused	Flexible

→ Arena: Circle the key aspects of your personality that you generally display and others would observe.

→ Façade: Which are the aspects of your personality that you prefer not to show and keep more private in certain situations? What types of situation might cause these aspects to be displayed? For example, when you are operating against a time deadline in a stressful environment, you may find that you become more dominant than you would like to be.

→ Blind spot: Think about three people who know you well and write their names down below. If you were to ask them what words from the table they would most identify with your personality, what do you think they would say, and why?

► Person 1

_____

_____

► Person 2

_____

_____

► Person 3

_____

_____

Now test it out! Show the three people you identified the list of words and ask them to give you their own answers. Note them down below and notice where there are similarities or differences.

_____

_____

_____

_____

_____

_____

_____

_____

THE UNKNOWN QUADRANT

The 'Unknown' quadrant of the Johari Window enables you to step out of your comfort zone and discover more about yourself. In the next chapter you will be able to learn more about unknown aspects of your personality by completing a trait-based assessment known as the Newcastle Personality Assessment. By using the results of this assessment, and perhaps sharing the information with other trusted contacts or asking others for feedback (as in the previous exercise), you increase your ability to reduce the area of unknown.

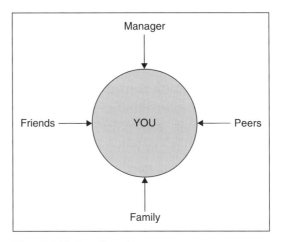

The 360° feedback process

Being willing to get different perspectives from others will give you a broader viewpoint that can be extremely helpful. Many HR and coaching professionals use 360° feedback processes to help executives at work to understand their behaviours from a variety of perspectives. Remember that others will base their perception of you on what they observe, and are likely to be unaware of all the elements that are unobservable.

INTERPRETING YOUR REPORT: TOP TIPS

▶ Check whether it's a type- or trait-based assessment – what is being measured?

▶ Remember that it is an objective assessment, not someone's opinion!

▶ Make sure the person delivering the feedback is a qualified consultant.

▶ Reports can often be quite detailed and you can feel overwhelmed with information; pace yourself and allow yourself time to digest the results properly.

▶ If you prefer to read through and reflect on the report before discussing it with a consultant, ask to obtain a copy prior to any conversation.

▶ Look for the 'outliers' in trait-based assessments, i.e. any scores that are extremely high or low. These characteristics are more likely to be either strengths or those that cause you to behave less effectively in times of stress or when your needs are not met.

▶ Share the results with others and find out whether their perception of you is similar.

▶ Think about what you are going to do differently as a result of the information received.

APPLYING THE LEARNING

Once you've read and understood your personality assessment report, the real value comes in being able to use that greater self-awareness to provide you with more choice and flexibility in how you behave in future situations.

Exercise 3.3

Have you ever found your thoughts matching any of the following statements?

→ My way is the best way to do this. ❏

→ My way is the only way. ❏

→ I'm okay – it's everyone else who has the problem. ❏

→ Most people are like me. ❏

→ I don't need to change. ❏

What these statements highlight is one way of viewing the world – the one through our own filters – and assuming that everyone else has the same beliefs and behaviours. That common misconception means that we limit our ability to be open to change and to accept others who display different characteristics of personality or behaviour from us.

Here is another set of statements. Which ones do you prefer?

→ There are many ways to do this. ❏

→ I'm okay and you're okay too. ❏

→ There's a broad range of personalities in the world, and I accept that others may be different from me. ❏

→ The only person I can change is me. ❏

→ If I always do what I've always done, I will always get what I've always got. ❏

PERSONALITY AND LEADERSHIP

Knowing that human beings are not all the same means learning to understand and appreciate different personality characteristics. This enables us to work more effectively with others as a result. If you have a position of leadership, it is even more important that you are able to use this knowledge in order to get the most effective performance possible from your team.

Although leaders may have 'positional' power, it is still vital that they can adapt their behaviour in order to be able to influence and effectively motivate others. Just telling people what to do works only in the short term and is not a sustainable leadership style.

Exercise 3.4

Think of the best leader you ever worked for – what characteristics did they have that made them the best?

_____

_____

_____

Think of the worst leader you ever worked for – what characteristics did they have that made them the worst?

_____

_____

_____

STRENGTHS – OR WEAKNESSES?

We often admire qualities in others that we have within ourselves. On the other hand, sometimes the characteristics that frustrate us in others are what we most need within ourselves.

This question of focusing on strengths is an important one to consider, particularly if the person receiving the results tends be self-critical, or feels inadequate. For people who may be self-critical, it's helpful to use the 3:1 ratio. This is to notice three positive qualities or characteristics that are valued by you or others, compared to every one that you may require the person to adapt.

Case study

Fiona worked in an event management company. She was a perfectionist and often spent hours longer than everyone else paying attention to every last detail in her arrangements. As a result of her behaviour, Fiona was not able to spend as much time on gaining new client business as her colleagues did.

As part of a company management programme, Fiona took a personality assessment. This gave her a very high score in conscientiousness (a tendency to show self-discipline and to work diligently towards measured achievements). When she talked through the results with the HR manager, Fiona was proud of her strength in that area and was surprised when the HR manager viewed it differently.

Fiona was told that she seemed to be unable to distinguish between tasks that had to be excellent and those where 'good enough' was acceptable. It was making her inefficient and causing stress among her colleagues because nothing was ever good enough.

When can a personality characteristic that you may view as a strength become a weakness?

_____

_____

In the case study on the previous page, what do you think would encourage Fiona to change her behaviour?

_____

_____

What can you learn from this case study about taking action when you have received feedback from a personality assessment?

_____

_____

....

Business coach Cathy Lasher devised the following 'Strengths, not overstrengths' tool as a way to help people maintain that balanced perspective.

Strengths, not overstrengths

Strength: Something you consistently do well	**Overstrength:** This is too much of a good thing. When you overdo the strength it becomes an overstrength
Avoidance: What you are determined to avoid (the opposite of your strength), the fear of which can push your strength into overstrength	**Balancing factor:** What you need to remember in order to keep the strength from becoming an overstrength

Here are two examples:

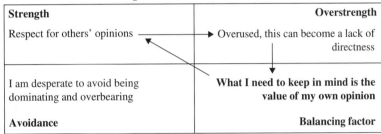

Strength	Overstrength
Respect for others' opinions	Overused, this can become a lack of directness
I am desperate to avoid being dominating and overbearing	**What I need to keep in mind is the value of my own opinion**
Avoidance	**Balancing factor**

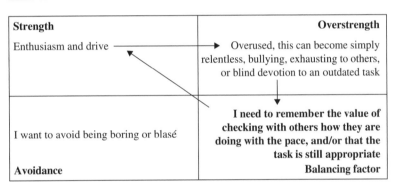

Strength	Overstrength
Enthusiasm and drive	Overused, this can become simply relentless, bullying, exhausting to others, or blind devotion to an outdated task
I want to avoid being boring or blasé	**I need to remember the value of checking with others how they are doing with the pace, and/or that the task is still appropriate**
Avoidance	**Balancing factor**

Try writing down your own example here:

Strength: *Write down a strength in this box.*	**Overstrength:** *What happens when it is too much of a good thing?*
Avoidance: *What are you determined to avoid (the opposite of your strength)?*	**Balancing factor:** *So what do you need to remember in order to keep the strength from becoming an overstrength?*

→ Willingness to change

The assessment process is part of the journey of change, and the good news is that these changes are not major ones, but small tweaks and improvements that can help you get what you want. Remember what you wrote down in the very first exercise? It was what you'd like to achieve as a result of reading this book.

That journey starts with the first small step. The secret of climbing a mountain, or painting a wall, is that it's a series of small and continuous activities that help take you towards the outcome you want. Every action is worth while, and although every brushstroke or step takes only a moment to do, if you are willing to continue with the actions, you can make the changes and get new results.

THE PROCESS OF CHANGE

As you are reading this book, or embarking on any type of change, it's likely that you will experience the change curve highlighted in the following diagram. The example is based on an individual taking a personality assessment and acting on its results. It shows their typical words and feelings.

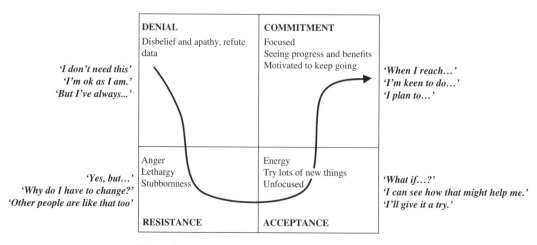

The change curve

What I have learned

REFLECTIONS

What are my thoughts, feelings and insights on what I have read so far?

YOUR JOURNEY

Summarize any actions you have identified as a result of reading this chapter.

Chapter	Actions
Introduction	
What is personality? 1 Personality: how temperament and character define you 2 Personality assessment tools and tests 3 How to use personality assessments	

Where to next?

This chapter has given you some tips on how to interpret personality assessments and how to recognize the difference between trait- and type-based assessments. It also explained the value of considering different perspectives when interpreting the information in a report, and how the mindset and willingness you bring to the process will make a difference to how you move forward.

In the next chapter the focus moves to carrying out a simple personality assessment to help you understand where you are. You will also learn more about the five dimensions of personality, which psychologists agree are the broad characteristics common in all human beings.

4 The five dimensions of personality

- ▶ What are the broad dimensions of personality that are common to everyone?
- ▶ How do I find out what my personality traits are?
- ▶ Why do I find some people's behaviour frustrating or annoying?
- ▶ Which aspects of my personality do I find most difficult to accept or to change?

In an effort to find out if there are any common dimensions of personality, researchers have studied and analysed the different traits that tend to occur consistently in how people describe themselves. A growing body of evidence highlights five broad dimensions of personality, often called the Big Five. They are all based on a continuum: that is, they go from one extreme to another. This chapter gives you the opportunity to assess yourself against these dimensions and find out which characteristics you identify with.

It is important to remember that the research discussed has been carried out by psychologists on the basis of probability. Because the research reflects the broad population, exceptions are always possible. As mentioned in previous chapters, many aspects of personality, such as attitudes and behaviours, are phenomena that cannot be precisely or easily measured.

→ What are the Big Five?

The Big Five, as they are known, are broad dimensions of personality traits. Most people will be found somewhere between the two polar ends of each dimension. The Big Five are:

▶ **Extraversion:** This includes characteristics of being talkative, energetic and assertive.

▶ **Neuroticism:** Also called emotional instability, this includes traits such as being tense, needy, moody and anxious.

▶ **Conscientiousness:** This includes traits such as being organized, thorough and having goal-directed behaviours.

▶ **Agreeableness:** This includes being kind, trusting, friendly and compassionate.

▶ **Openness to experience:** This includes traits such as having wide interests and being imaginative and insightful.

The following Newcastle Personality Assessment allows you to assess yourself against these broad five personality dimensions. This assessment is very broad. If you want more detail, there are some more specific assessments on the market which are described in Chapter 2.

Exercise 4.1

BEHAVIOUR AND PERSONALITY

In the following table you will see a list of descriptions of behaviours and thoughts. Read through them and rate to what extent they are typically how you would think and behave.

Behaviour	Not like me at all	Partly unlike me	Neither one nor another	Partly like me	Very like me	Score
1 Starting a conversation with a stranger						
2 Making sure others are comfortable and happy						
3 Creating an artwork, a piece of writing or a piece of music						
4 Preparing things well in advance						
5 Feeling blue or depressed						
6 Planning parties or social events						
7 Insulting people						
8 Thinking about philosophical or spiritual questions						
9 Letting things get into a mess						
10 Feeling stressed or worried						
11 Using difficult words						
12 Sympathizing with others' feelings						

Record a score for each of your answers, using the following key.

For all questions other than 7 and 9	For questions 7 and 9
Not like me at all = 1	Not like me at all = 5
Partly unlike me = 2	Partly unlike me = 4
Neither one nor another = 3	Neither one nor another = 3
Partly like me = 4	Partly like me = 2
Very like me = 5	Very like me = 1

Now work out your score for the five dimensions of personality by adding up your score from the individual questions as shown below.

Dimension	To calculate score	Your total
Extraversion	Q1 + Q6	
Neuroticism	Q5 + Q10	
Conscientiousness	Q4 + Q9	
Agreeableness	Q2 + Q7 + Q12	
Openness	Q3 + Q8 + Q11	

Review your scores and interpret your rating below (which is according to the whole population).

Scores	Extraversion	Neuroticism	Conscientiousness
Low scores = 2, 3, 4			
Low/medium scores = 5 and 6			
Medium/high scores = 7 and 8			
High scores = 9 and 10			

Agreeableness

Low scores = 10 or less; low/medium scores = 11 and 12; medium/high scores = 13; high = 14 and 15. There is a difference in gender on these scores: for men, 9 or less is a low score compared to other men, 10 and 11 are low/medium, 12 and 13 are medium/high, 14 and 15 are high. For women, 11 or less is a low score compared to other women, 12 and 13 are low/medium, 14 is medium/high, 15 is high. About 16% of women and 4% of men score a maximum of 15.

Openness to experience

Low scores = 8 or less; low/medium scores = 9 and 10; medium/high scores = 11 and 12; high scores = 13, 14, 15.

··

→ Using your scores

Throughout the rest of the book there will be exercises that will help you gain more insight about your personality by using the scores in this questionnaire. If your scores are different from what you thought about yourself, it is helpful to reflect on situations you have experienced in the past and how you behaved. Is your behaviour consistent? How would your friends describe you? Collecting feedback from a number of sources and different situations can help you to reflect on when, and with whom, perhaps different aspects of your personality appear.

Following on from the previous chapters that outlined the four broad areas of focus on External, Internal, People and Tasks, it can be helpful to consider how the Big Five dimensions of personality relate to these areas.

→ Extraversion

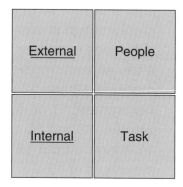

External	People
Internal	Task

Extraversion

The first characteristic, extraversion, is primarily concerned with the two areas of Internal and External which are underlined in the diagram above. Extraversion relates to the degree to which we get energized by the outside world, i.e. the world outside ourselves. Typically, people with a high level of extraversion love social events like parties, family gatherings and big occasions where there are a number of people involved because they typically get energy from being with others.

At the other end of the spectrum, people with a low level of extraversion prefer to be interested and become energized by what's going on inside themselves, i.e. their inner mental world. They are likely to be more reflective and think things through before speaking; hence they can come across to others as quiet. Typical activities may be completing a crossword puzzle or thinking about how to solve a problem.

Exercise 4.2

ARE YOU AN EXTRAVERT?

Imagine that you have had a really busy week at work and you want to do something to unwind and recharge your batteries.

→ Write down the type of activity you most enjoy. Why do you enjoy it?

_____

→ Write down the type of activity you least enjoy. Why do you not enjoy it?

_____

→ Review your score from the Newcastle Personality Assessment (Exercise 4.1) and whether the result was low, medium or high.

_____

High extraversion: you enjoy being around people and activities are likely to be energetic. You least enjoy solitary activities that require a lot of thinking.

Low extraversion: you enjoy time alone to reflect and think things through. You least enjoy being in large groups of people, and are more likely to have a few close friends.

Medium extraversion: you enjoy both being around people and spending time on your own.

How does your score correlate with what you wrote down as an enjoyable activity?

_____

_____

· ·

→ # Neuroticism

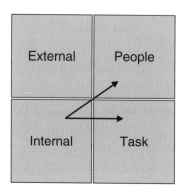

Neuroticism

Of the Big Five, neuroticism may seem like a less 'positive' trait than agreeableness, openness, extraversion and conscientiousness. Yet it is important to understand what this trait is and how it may impact on our mindset and behaviour.

If we relate it to the other four traits above, it is likely that this trait will demonstrate how an individual reacts from an internal perspective towards people and tasks. For example, in their inner world they may be worried that they could upset their manager if they tell them they are struggling to complete a report on time. Rather than checking whether this is reality, they assume the worst and get even more stressed. So the manifestation of their focus on their internal world shows up in how they approach people and tasks.

Exercise 4.3

ARE YOU NEUROTIC?

Think about how you tend to view the world – would you describe yourself as a glass half-empty or glass half-full sort of person?

Neuroticism may be related to the glass half-empty perspective as people with high levels tend to be more pessimistic. For example, they suffer more often than others from feelings of anxiety, guilt, envy and anger, and are more likely to have more depressed moods. On an everyday basis they might be prone to what some would describe as 'making a mountain out of a molehill', i.e. they experience trivial frustrations as major obstacles.

Individuals with high levels of neuroticism tend to be worrisome, emotional, vulnerable, self-conscious, self-pitying and temperamental, while those with lower levels tend to be more calm, even-tempered, unemotional, self-satisfied, comfortable and hardy.

Exercise 4.4

HOW DO YOU APPROACH CHANGE?

Read the descriptions below of how George and Madeleine tried to find another job. Highlight the elements that you relate to.

George was fed up. His job was no longer satisfying and so he decided it was time for a change. He tidied up his CV, called a few recruitment agencies and told them about his capabilities and the type of job he was looking for. A few days later he was invited for interview. As he drove there, there was a big car pile-up on the motorway, which caused him to be delayed. George was not too fazed and rang ahead to explain the situation. When he eventually arrived, he looked relaxed, smiled at the interviewers and approached the situation calmly and with ease. After all, he asked himself, what was the worst that could happen?

Madeleine was unhappy in her job and had started to consider a change. However, she was worried about several things. What if she applied for a job in a company she really wanted to work in, and then did not come across well in an interview and did not get any further? That would be too much to bear. Then she began to get nervous that her CV showed that she had been in her job for ten years. Others would think she had no drive or interest in her career. Eventually she decided just to stay put, because it was going to be too stressful to make a change. Then she felt bad about not being brave enough to take action.

Now answer these questions.

→Which person do you relate to most?

_____

→What are the downsides of each person's approach?

_____

_____

_____

→What could they do differently?

_____

_____

_____

Recognizing whether you score high or low on the neuroticism trait continuum will help you understand your current behaviour. In the following chapters, you will learn how you can adapt your behaviour to get the results you want.

→ Conscientiousness

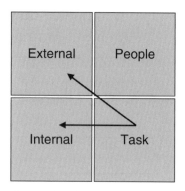

Conscientiousness

Of all the five dimensions, conscientiousness is the most reliable predictor of occupational success. In general, the higher your score in conscientiousness the better you will do, where all other things are equal. People with a high level of conscientiousness tend to be trustworthy, dependable, efficient and well organized, while people at the low end of the spectrum are likely to be flexible, easy-going and impulsive. We tend to think about people being conscientious in relation to a task, and how they display that is likely to be either external (in how they express themselves) or internal (how they reflect inwardly and gain their ability to be organized).

Exercise 4.5

ORGANIZED OR FLEXIBLE?

Think about a situation where you were required to achieve a task, for example invite a friend to dinner, complete a report or organize a meeting. Write down below how you achieved the task and the timeline of activities.

_____

_____

Review what you have written in terms of the following questions.

→ When were you energized to take action?

_____

→ Did you have a plan before you started?

_____

→ If changes occurred along the way, how did you react?

_____

Think about what this tells you about your approach. Do you generally prefer to plan and be organized, or do you prefer to leave things until the last minute and adapt as you go?

_____

Now examine the same situation from another person's perspective. It may be the person coming to dinner, the individual receiving the report or the attendee at the meeting.

→ What might they say about how you behave?

_____

→ How would you like to be seen by others?

_____

_____

If you have a high level of conscientiousness, you have the ability to be organized and dependable. However, when plans or situations alter, how adaptable are you in coping with change? People with a high level of conscientiousness often find it hard to accept that the result is 'good enough' because of their desire for perfection. At the other end of the spectrum are those people who are easy-going and flexible, but who sometimes find it difficult to be structured.

Exercise 4.6

Read the following case study.

Tom liked to keep in touch with his friends. At the weekend he would find out what they were doing and then wait until the last minute to make a decision. His friends grew to realize that they could not rely on him because, if he found a better activity, he would suddenly change his plans and often leave his friends feeling let down or disappointed.

While Tom did not like to be tied down to a firm plan, he began to realize that he was never really spending quality time with anyone, but just mooching on from one thing to the next, and it was getting to be unsatisfying. His desire for freedom and flexibility had its downsides and he needed to change.

What would you suggest that Tom does differently?

_____

_____

As we go through this book, you will learn more about the pluses and minuses of each of the characteristics, and you will be able to use some practical tools to help you adapt your behaviour in order to achieve different results.

→ Agreeableness

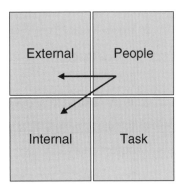

Agreeableness

We tend to associate agreeableness with the ability to give energy to people; hence the trait could simply be described as either a focus on 'self' (internal) or on 'others' (external). Those with a high score for agreeableness are likely to be friendly, co-operative, trusting and compassionate. They are likely to pay close attention to others' mental states and to consider them in their choice of behaviour, whereas those with a low score are likely to be cold-hearted, hostile and not concerned with the wellbeing of others.

This dimension is the one that has a gender difference, with women tending to have higher levels of agreeableness than men.

WIN–WIN

The topic of negotiation is relevant when it comes to agreeableness as your approach (self or other) will influence the outcome. There are normally six possible outcomes in a negotiation situation and they will be influenced by your attitude (internal) and behaviours (external). The outcomes are:

1 **Win–lose:** 'I'll get my way; you won't get yours.'

2 **Lose–win:** 'You'll probably get your way; I won't get mine.'

3 **Lose–lose:** 'If I can't get my way, I'll make sure you can't get yours.'

4 **Win–lose:** 'I'll secure my way and leave you to secure yours.'

5 **Win–win:** 'It's not my way or your way – let's look for a better way.'

6 **No deal:** 'If we can't find a way that benefits us both, let's agree to disagree.'

Examples of situations needing negotiation are:

▶ getting your child to go to bed

▶ agreeing the time your teenagers get home at night

▶ discussing with your partner where you go on holiday

▶ negotiating price with a new supplier.

Exercise 4.7

NEGOTIATING AND YOUR PERSONALITY

The following questionnaire from Quantum Corporate Coaching can help you assess to what degree you have an interest in others compared to your own interests.

Here are 12 paired items. Read each pair of statements and put a tick beside the statement that most closely applies to you. If both statements in the pair apply, mark the one that applies to you most, however marginal the difference.

1	When negotiating, I prefer to keep my 'bottom line' to myself.	2	When negotiating, I prefer to avoid having a predetermined 'bottom line'.
3	I prefer to go into discussions with a general goal and be flexible about my specific objective within that goal.	4	I prefer to go into discussions with a fixed objective in mind.
5	I rarely ask other people about their objectives.	6	I frequently ask other people about their objectives
7	I often feel determined to get my own way.	8	I often feel determined to find a better way, even if it means compromising.
9	When negotiating, I prefer to reach an agreement, however difficult it might be.	10	When negotiating, if I can't find an acceptable outcome I prefer to agree to disagree.
11	I prefer to explore and search for common ground.	12	I prefer to push ahead and do my best to achieve my objective.
13	At the start of discussions, I tend to be open about what I hope to achieve.	14	At the start of discussions, I tend to keep what I hope to achieve to myself.
15	In negotiations, my primary aim is to reach an amicable agreement.	16	In negotiations, my primary aim is to reach an effective outcome.
17	Whenever my opinions differ from other people's, I like to explore the reasons for the differences.	18	Whenever my opinions differ from other people's, I try even harder to persuade them to accept my point of view.
19	I often feel compelled to win concessions from other people.	20	I feel that the best solutions do not require concessions from anyone.
21	I often find that people take up entrenched positions and refuse to budge.	22	I find that people are prepared to divulge the reasons why they have taken up a position.
23	When negotiating, I confront the problem, not the person.	24	When negotiating, I am either confrontational or conciliatory with people, depending on who they are.

Go through your responses to the questionnaire items and indicate them in the appropriate boxes below. Be careful because the sequence below will not always replicate the sequence of items in the questionnaire.

1	☐		2	☐
4	☐		3	☐
5	☐		6	☐
7	☐		8	☐
9	☐		10	☐
12	☐		11	☐
14	☐		13	☐
15	☐		16	☐
18	☐		17	☐
19	☐		20	☐
21	☐		22	☐
24	☐		23	☐
Total	☐		Total	☐

Confrontational

COMPETITIVE

Score

Win–win

CO-OPERATIVE

Score

Interpreting your score

If you have a high level of agreeableness, it is likely that your score for a win–win approach will exceed your score for a confrontational approach. To give you a comparison, below are the norms based on the win–win scores obtained by 150 North American and British managers drawn from a cross-section of different organizations and functions.

Score for win–win	Interpretation
12	A very high score, only obtained by 10 per cent of the managers in the sample
10–11	Also a high score, obtained by the next 20 per cent of the managers in the sample
8–9	Moderate scores, achieved by the middle 40 per cent of the sample
6–7	Relatively low scores, indicating a tendency to be more confrontational than win–win
0–5	Very low scores for win–win, obtained by the bottom 10 per cent of the sample

People with a high level of competitive behaviour are more likely to have a lower score in agreeableness and may seek to dominate the other person in negotiations. They are likely to regard others as adversaries, and will show little interest in another person's needs. Their focus is likely to be on short-term gain for themselves.

At the other end of the spectrum, individuals with a high level of co-operative behaviour are more likely to have a higher score in agreeableness and be more 'other' focused. They tend to be more flexible and to seek solutions by mutual problem solving. Information is likely to be shared as they are open and trusting. They are more likely to ask questions than make statements.

In Chapter 8 you will be able to understand more about how the dimension of agreeableness has relevance when navigating other people's personality traits.

→ Openness to experience

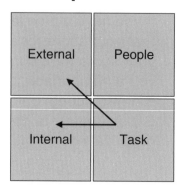

Openness

The fifth dimension – of openness – is really related to one's internal and external attitudes and behaviours in relation to new experiences, which can be task related.

People who have a high score for openness are likely to have a preference for variety, to have an active imagination and curiosity, and to have greater aesthetic sensitivity than others. At the other end of the spectrum, those who score low for openness are considered to be more conventional and traditional in their outlook and behaviour. They prefer familiar routines to new experience and generally have a narrower range of interests than other people.

Exercise 4.8

In order to gain more insight into the characteristic of openness, think about which one of each of the following pairs of statements describes your preference. They relate to different aspects of arranging a team-building event for a group of people in your organization. If you think they are both relevant, you'll need to decide which one would be of higher priority.

Programme

- ▶ coming up with new ideas and concepts ❏
- ▶ finding out what has worked before and replicating it ❏

Selecting a venue

- ▶ somewhere tried and tested and that has been recommended ❏
- ▶ a new venue that looks great on the website and is a bit 'different' ❏

Room set-up

- ▶ not that important – more about what's on the agenda ❏
- ▶ the right environment will make all the difference ❏

Now review your answers and consider whether they would be different if you were taking part in the event yourself.

_____

_____

What does this tell you about your level of openness to experience?

_____

_____

Consider whether your openness to experience is similar in each of the areas below:

→ Going on holiday

_____

→ Eating out

_____

→ Starting a new project at work

_____

→ Your expectations about your career path

_____

→ Meeting new people

_____

All five dimensions of personality described in this chapter have highlighted the 'extremes' of behaviour at each end of the spectrum, and for many people there is not a clear-cut score for any of them. That's okay; the important point to consider is that your personality influences your ability to achieve success in whatever way that may be for you.

Exercise 4.9

Having carried out the exercises in this chapter, review the following:

→ What do you think are the broad dimensions of your personality?

_____

_____

_____

→ How does this insight help you in relation to what you want to do/be in the future?

_____

_____

_____

→ Which particular aspects should you focus on?

_____

_____

_____

What I have learned

REFLECTIONS

What are my thoughts, feelings and insights on what I have read so far?

YOUR JOURNEY

Summarize any actions you have identified as a result of reading this chapter.

Chapter	Actions
Introduction How to use this workbook	
What is personality? 1 Personality: how temperament and character define you 2 Personality assessment tools and tests 3 How to use personality assessments	
Assessing where you are 4 The five dimensions of personality	

Where to next?

Now that you have an understanding of the five dimensions of personality and how they apply to you and others, you can consider how these various personality traits may influence behaviour. In the next chapter you will learn how your personality impacts on goal setting and achievement. This will help you understand why you behave as you do and how you can do things differently in order to get a different outcome in future.

5 *Your personality, goal setting and achievement*

- ▶ *I tend to avoid goal setting. Why is that?*
- ▶ *I am good at setting my own goals, but not so motivated when my boss gives me something to achieve. How can I be more motivated to work on her goals?*
- ▶ *I want to achieve a really difficult goal but I am not sure how to start.*
- ▶ *I start working towards a goal and then get distracted. What aspect of my personality do I need to adapt?*

The word 'goals' can cause interesting reactions. Some people thrive on setting goals and working towards them, while others detest the idea of making a commitment to achieve an outcome. They want the freedom to change their minds along the way, or fear that they will be viewed as a failure if they don't achieve a stated goal.

In this chapter you will learn about the relationship between different types of personalities and the issue of goals and achieving outcomes. By understanding this, the insight will give you practical ways that you can adapt your behaviour in future in order to get the results you want.

> 'A goal is a dream with a deadline.'
>
> Napoleon Hill, author (1883–1970)

According to Napoleon Hill in his classic book *Think and Grow Rich* (first published in 1937 and still in print), thoughts are things and they are also 'powerful when they are mixed with definiteness of purpose, persistence, and a burning desire for their translation into riches, or other material objects'. Even if you think you don't like, or rarely set, goals, you are likely to be already doing so unwittingly via your thoughts, and then wondering why you got the outcome you did.

Even if you dislike the word 'goal' and are fed up with hearing about SMART objectives, it's important to understand how the different dimensions of your personality impact on the different stages of goal setting and achievement. It is your choice as to whether you use the term goal, objective or anything else; but what is important is the appreciation and understanding of how you can adapt your personality in the pursuit of achieving what you want, by maximizing your strengths or modifying your behaviour.

Exercise 5.1

THOUGHTS AND OUTCOMES

When we focus on something we 'don't want', we are just as likely to get it because our brain cannot distinguish between real or imagined thoughts, and then our subconscious works towards making what we have focused on become a reality. The following case study illustrates this.

Max was preparing to make a presentation to an investor in order to secure investment funding for his business. Being highly conscientious, Max was well organized and meticulous over the details of his slides and practised to ensure that he spoke for no more than the allocated time. However, he kept worrying that he would say something stupid and that everyone would laugh and he would look embarrassed.

Guess what happened? With that thought implanted in his mind, he made a mistake in pronouncing the investor's name, and then his 'dream became a reality'.

Can you think of a time where you have ended with an outcome that you did not want as a result of what you were thinking about?

_____

_____

_____

→ # Factors that influence goal setting

Three factors likely to influence your goal setting are:

▶ the **difficulty** of the task – as you perceive it

▶ your **interest** in doing it – how you feel about it/your passion for doing it

▶ your **goal orientation** – as you believe it to be.

DIFFICULTY

How you perceive a task, in relation to the amount of effort you may need to put in, will influence how you set goals. This perception draws upon our objective assessment of what is required and an assessment of our ability.

Exercise 5.2

Imagine you were asked by your manager to prepare a presentation to the rest of your company – which has 50 employees – on your greatest weaknesses.

→ How would you rate this in terms of difficulty?

_____

→ How would you objectively assess the task?

_____

_____

→ How would you assess your ability to do it?

_____

_____

INTEREST

If you have a high level of interest (feeling real passion) in a task to be achieved, then it is far more likely that you will have an emotional connection to it. When setting goals, it is therefore important to assess to what degree you are interested in achieving the outcome.

Exercise 5.3

Rate yourself on a scale of 1 to 10 (1 = no interest, 10 = keen) on your level of interest to achieve the task outlined in the previous exercise (delivering a presentation about your weaknesses).

_____

→ What does this score tell you?

_____

_____

→ What would have to happen in order to increase your level of interest?

_____

_____

GOAL ORIENTATION

Your attraction to a goal will be driven by your belief in it. According to researchers Horvath, Herleman and McKie of Clemson University in South Carolina, there are three different types of goal orientation linked to your personality, which are:

▶ **mastery goal** orientation, where the focus in on learning and improving ability

▶ **performance approach** orientation, where the focus is on demonstrating competence

▶ **performance avoidance** orientation, where the focus is on trying to avoid revealing a lack of competence.

Think of it as doing the high jump. Mastery behaviour would be to put the bar up higher than you have jumped before to see if you can improve or learn more, because you believe you can or should do it. Performance approach behaviour would be to jump at the same height as you have achieved before and that you know you can do comfortably, to demonstrate your capability, i.e. your belief that it will lead to a safe result. Performance avoidance behaviour would be to develop an injury just prior to taking the jump because you don't believe you can do it!

If a person has a performance avoidance orientation (trying to avoid revealing their incompetence), they may have a perception that somehow their capability will be evaluated. This is a self-limiting behaviour in that it is likely that the person will end up procrastinating and setting goals below their true potential.

Case study

Helen did not like having to speak in public. She always got nervous, with sweaty palms and a dry throat. From these signals Helen concluded that she was no good at public speaking, and so she avoided situations where she might have to 'demonstrate her incompetence', as she saw it. As a result, Helen missed out on opportunities at work to make presentations to the management team on some of her interesting projects. This ultimately affected her promotion chances, as she was not allowing her talent to be seen by the decision makers and influencers.

Eventually, Helen realized that she couldn't accept her belief in 'That's just how I am' any longer. She consulted a coach, who was able to help her realize that she was observing her physical reaction to the stressful situation and incorrectly attributing it to her ability. Once she recognized this, she began to focus on noting down her successes rather than the times when she felt incompetent. This new approach (based on the concept of appreciative enquiry) helped her to build her belief in 'I can do it'.

'No one can make you feel inferior without your consent.'

Eleanor Roosevelt, US First Lady (1884–1962)

Exercise 5.4

Reflect on two recent situations that required the achievement of goals. Note down your thoughts in the table below.

Situation A	A goal that you set for yourself	A goal that someone else set for you
1 What was your goal orientation? (a) to learn and improve (b) to demonstrate competence (c) to avoid being seen as incompetent		
2 What does this tell you about your personality in relation to goal setting?		

Situation B	A goal that you set for yourself	A goal that someone else set for you
1 What was your goal orientation? (a) to learn and improve (b) to demonstrate competence (c) to avoid being seen as incompetent		
2 What does this tell you about your personality in relation to goal setting?		

→ The process of goal setting and achievement

Now that you have established how your personality may affect your ability to set goals that enable you to step out of your comfort zone, as described earlier in this chapter, it's worth giving some consideration to what happens next.

You identify an outcome that you have to or want to achieve. But how do you make it happen, and how does your personality help you or cause you problems?

Are you the type of person who is great at defining what you want to achieve, making a plan, taking action and achieving results? Or maybe you are spontaneous, grabbing opportunities that come along, enjoying the experience and being happy with the outcome, whatever it is? Alternatively, you might be one of those people who loathe the word goal because it reminds you of being tied into a commitment to achieve an outcome, and if you don't manage it you feel you have failed, so it's better not to start.

The next exercise explores what actually happens in your reality to enable you to accomplish outcomes. Having already learned about the three factors that influence goal setting, you will now gain more detailed knowledge of how you achieved your eventual outcomes.

Exercise 5.5

Write down three significant accomplishments that you have achieved recently.

1 _____

2 _____

3 _____

→ What happened in order for you to achieve those things? Were they planned or unplanned?

_____

_____

_____

_____

_____

_____

→ As you went through the experience of going towards achieving each outcome, did your views on goal setting and achievement change at all?

_____

→ Did you get the results you expected or were they unexpected?

_____

→ To what degree did you change your behaviour the next time you focused on an outcome?

_____

_____

→ What do you say to yourself about the idea of setting and working towards goals (e.g. there's no point because I don't follow through)?

_____

_____

→ What do you now believe about the value of goals?

_____

_____

→ If there was one aspect of your personality that you would like to change in relation to this activity of goal setting and achievement, what would it be?

_____

By answering the above questions, you should have gained greater insight into how your personality impacts this process and what you may like to accept or change.

→ The positive effect of goal setting

According to a study carried out by Dominican University of California, people who wrote down their goals accomplished significantly more than those who did not write them down. In addition, those who sent weekly progress reports to their friends as well as writing their goals down accomplished significantly more than those who either had unwritten goals, wrote their goals, formulated action commitments or sent those action commitments to a friend.

So there is value in doing two things when you want to achieve a goal:

1 Write it down.

2 Make a public commitment to a friend and keep them posted on progress.

The idea of making a public commitment or even writing a goal down may make you feel uncomfortable, however, because facets of your personality cause you to resist taking these actions as they are in conflict with how you prefer to behave. But life will force you to plan. The longer you wait to do it, the fewer resources you will have and the more dissatisfying your choices will be.

Once you have used the table opposite to review how the different dimensions of your personality are likely to affect your motivation and interest in goal setting, carry out the next reflective exercise in order to ascertain specifically which part of the process of goal setting you enjoy, detest or don't do.

Committing to your goals

The five dimensions of personality	Low score	High score
Extraversion	With your focus on 'inner world', it can be difficult to share a goal with others until it has been thought through sufficiently.	With a preference to talk, you have probably shared and discussed your ideas already with several people, particularly if you also have a high score for openness to experience.
Neuroticism	You are likely to feel confident to write down your goals and make a commitment to share them with others.	The cycle of thoughts may relate to: • What may happen if I write it down? • Will it go wrong? • Then what will others think of me? • I'd better not make the commitment.
Conscientiousness	You like freedom and independence and don't want to be tied down to something written down because that makes you feel restricted. You are likely to write down a goal 'when you want to', rather than just because others are doing it too.	You are likely to be committed and well organized, with a list of goals thought through in detail. Any resistance to writing down a goal may be related to the desire to get it 'right' before committing it to paper or sharing it with others.
Agreeableness	You are likely to be focused on your goals and what you want to achieve. If you think it will help you to write down your goals, you are likely to do it, seizing the opportunity. If sharing your goals with others could help you, you will be motivated to do it.	You pay more attention to the needs of others than your own. That strength can get in the way of you ever making time to satisfy your own goals and needs.
Openness to experience	Ever practical and cautious, writing down a goal will enable you to take some useful action, and you are likely to be good at following up on a regular basis with the person with whom you committed to share progress.	You love new ideas and concepts but you can get caught up in an idea rather than the concrete steps required to make the idea into a goal and then into reality.

Exercise 5.6

GOAL-SETTING ACTIVITIES

Read the list of activities related to setting and achieving goals in the table opposite.

Rate each one on a scale of 1 to 5, according to how much you enjoy the activity and how often you do it.

Then use your results to answer the following questions.

→ What are the activities in goal setting that you really enjoy?

_____

_____

_____

→ What is the reason you enjoy them?

_____

_____

_____

→ What are the activities you don't enjoy?

_____

_____

_____

Activities in setting and achieving goals	Rate on scale of 1 (don't enjoy) to 5 (really enjoy)	Rate on scale of 1 (do it rarely or never) to 5 (do it regularly)
Coming up with ideas and options		
Setting myself challenging goals that will take me out of my comfort zone		
Writing down goals, e.g. to take up archery		
Identifying the measure of success, e.g. booked on to a course		
Clarifying the 'why' behind the goal, e.g. to find out if I can do it		
Start taking action towards achieving the goal		
Getting others to encourage and support me		
Reporting on progress to others		
Rewarding myself along the way to keep motivated		
Having milestones to focus on		
Focusing on the problems and risks and working out how to solve them		
Getting to the end outcome as I had planned		
Reviewing why things happened as they did		
Putting that learning into practice in future		

➜ What aspects of your personality most often cause you issues when setting and achieving goals?

_____

_____

_____

➜ Which part of the goal-setting and achievement process would you like to be able to do more effectively?

_____

_____

_____

Now think about how often you carry out these activities, because sometimes the more you do something the easier it becomes, as long as you have found a way to make it work for you personality.

➜ What elements of your personality do you now accept or wish to change or manage differently?

_____

_____

_____

What I have learned

REFLECTIONS

What are my thoughts, feelings and insights on what I have read so far?

YOUR JOURNEY

Summarize any actions you have identified as a result of reading this chapter.

Chapter	Actions
Introduction	
Understanding the topic 1 Personality: how temperament and character define you 2 Personality assessment tools and tests 3 How to use personality assessments	
Assessing where you are 4 The five dimensions of personality 5 Your personality, goal setting and achievement	

Where to next?

This chapter has outlined how different aspects of personality impact in different ways on the process of setting and achieving goals. In the next chapter you will learn how to set goals that motivate you, regardless of your personality preferences. You may not even wish to describe them as goals, but that's fine because you will understand what is going to motivate you instead to move towards a result or outcome.

6 *How to set goals that will motivate you*

- ▶ What do you want to achieve that is new or that you have not been able to achieve already?
- ▶ What do you want to achieve that will really stretch your capabilities?
- ▶ What type of goal or outcome usually motivates you?
- ▶ What normally stops you from achieving your goals?

By now you should have a clearer understanding of how you tend to respond in relation to the issue of goals, and in this chapter you will learn some tips and techniques on how to set goals that will motivate you and help you to achieve more. Using the five dimensions of personality as the framework for setting your goals, you will be able to learn new behaviours that should lead you to the outcomes you want.

No matter what the innate characteristics of your personality are, you can apply new knowledge to enable you to adopt new ways of behaving that should lead to you getting a different result.

→ The stages of goal setting

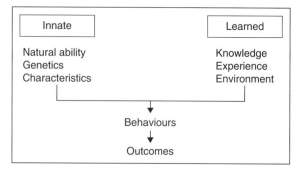

How personality impacts on outcomes

During the different stages of the goal-setting process, each of the five dimensions of personality can have an impact. Before you work through the exercises in this chapter, refer back to Chapter 4 to re-familiarize yourself with the five dimensions of personality and remind yourself of your own scores.

Exercise 6.1

Note down your scores from the Newcastle Personality Questionnaire from Chapter 4, and remind yourself of whether your scores are high or low here:

- ▶ Extraversion =   Low/high
- ▶ Neuroticism =   Low/high
- ▶ Conscientiousness =   Low/high
- ▶ Agreeableness =   Low/high
- ▶ Openness =   Low/high

Dimension	Low score	High score
Extraversion	Reserved, solitary	Outgoing, sociable, energetic
Neuroticism	Confident, secure	Sensitive, nervous
Conscientiousness	Easy-going, unstructured	Efficient, organized
Agreeableness	Suspicious, unfriendly	Friendly, compassionate
Openness to experience	Consistent, cautious	Inventive, curious

Individuals tend to carry out four broad steps in the process of setting the goal itself. They then take a fifth step, which is to begin taking action towards achieving the outcome by sharing the goal with others. The steps are outlined below and each one tends to have particular relevance to a different personality dimension. Chapter 7 covers the final step, 'Share with others', in more detail, putting the positioning of your goals in a wider context and considering external influences.

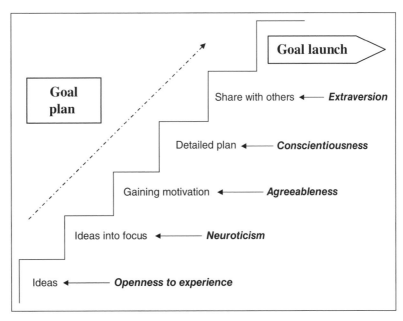

Steps in the goal-setting process

Exercise 6.2

Refer to the previous chart and in the table below tick the steps in the goal-setting process that you enjoy most and give the reason why. Avoid simply saying 'because it's easy', but try to think about what attributes or aspects make it enjoyable.

Step	Enjoy/dislike?	Why?
1 Ideas		
2 Ideas into focus		
3 Gaining motivation		
4 Detailed plan		
5 Share with others		

Next, mark with an X those you find least enjoyable, and again give the reason why.

This chapter considers the steps in goal setting in terms of personality traits and types. For each step, useful tips and techniques are explained for both high scorers in that particular personality dimension (as a strength overused can become a weakness) and those with a low score who may wish to develop that area of their personality.

→ Step 1: Ideas

Coming up with creative ideas can be exhilarating and, if you have a high score in openness to experience, it's likely that you really enjoy this part of the goal-setting process. It can often be linked to right-brain thinking, with its focus on expressive and creative tasks, as opposed to left-brain thinking, which is more focused on logical thinking, analysis and accuracy.

Without the characteristic of openness, some of the world's best-known pieces of music or art may not have been created. It's the ability to come up with concepts or ideas for 'what's possible' and not to be constrained by 'what is'.

For example, the concept of a long-haul, low-cost airline was started in the 1970s by the American domestic carrier Southwest, which had the sole objective of offering cheap airfares to consumers. Their original low-cost model was based on the concept of unrestricted and low-price fares, point-to-point high-frequency routes, booking via call centres, using the same types of aircraft across the fleet, and short sectors flying to airports with short turnaround times. At the time no one else in the USA was doing this, so they had to imagine what was possible and then take the idea from concept through all the other stages to make it happen.

At the other end of the scale, those who have a low score in openness to experience may find the activity of coming up with new concepts and generating ideas quite difficult.

You can try out many different activities to develop your creativity and generate ideas, such as those described on the following pages.

Exercise 6.3

REVERSE BRAINSTORMING

This activity is good for generating new ideas, and is particularly useful for those who have low scores in openness to experience. There are worksheets at the back of the book to use for this activity.

Decide what the task/problem/issue is that you want to generate new and different ideas for. Frame a question that captures your task/problem/issue in a form such as 'How can I...?' For example, 'How can I get organized to run before work?' Write your question in the space below.

_____

_____

Now write a question that is the reverse of it. For example, if your problem is 'How can I get organized to run before work?' the reverse might be 'How can I ensure I have no spare time before work?'

_____

List as many ideas as you can for how you could make sure the reverse statement happens. For the example given above, you could get up five minutes before you are due to leave, stay up late the night before so you are tired, make a packed lunch, talk to the family over breakfast, walk the neighbour's dog or spend 15 minutes in the shower.

_____

_____

Next, take those ideas and reverse them back again. For the example above, you could be organized to leave five minutes before you are due to leave, go to bed early, buy lunch at work, eat breakfast alone, run with the neighbour's dog or spend five minutes in the shower.

_____

_____

_____

_____

_____

Review the new ideas you have generated and see whether any of them will help you to address your problem.

_____

_____

By considering the reverse ideas first (the opposite side of the problem), did you find that it helped you to counter any resistance you had? Also, as you began to re-orientate the reverse statements into solutions, did you find yourself beginning to evaluate options more constructively and optimistically?

CURIOSITY

Being curious helps you ask questions and expand your thinking, especially if you can be unconstrained and not limit your curiosity. Take an event at your work that surprised you. This could be a good or bad event , such as a curtailed contract, a sudden interest in one of your services or products, or a colleague getting promotion unexpectedly. Think about all the circumstances around this event, and ask questions about what has affected what.

MULTIPLE USES

We commonly use things for their intended purpose and nothing else, but most things offer a wealth of possibilities. Ask questions: for example, what could you do with a biro top, apart from baling out a budgie's water trough? Think of objects as alterable.

OPEN MIND

There are always a number of ways to look at the same situation. Less creative people tend to see only one. Try to look at every viewpoint you can think of: see a situation from the perspective of your manager, of the person who sits next to you, of your neighbours and of your mother or a sibling. This brings out the realization that there really are many sides to one coin and, once you start thinking like that, creativity starts happening.

RANDOM WORDS

Start with any word picked from the dictionary. Think about what that word means, and all the things it could mean or suggest. Spread out to other associations. For example, start with the word cheese. You could start with its nutritional value, and the way cheese can be created from a liquid and become solid. There is versatility – there are dozens of different products that are all cheese. There are different colours and flavours, caused by willingness to introduce new items of many types, like onions, pineapple and whisky. What possibilities does this bring to mind in relation to your ideas?

DIVERSIFY YOUR STIMULI

Obtaining ideas and thoughts from sources that are not in your normal world can provide great stimulus to improve or possibly make a step change to your thinking. This intellectual cross-pollination can offer you new directions into which to take your goals, so be alert and open minded about developing your cross-functional skills and network. Get to know people who spark your imagination. Become a lifelong learner: take classes not related to your work and try new things in your personal life such as a hobby or an new interest.

Exercise 6.4

Try each of the six creative methods described above and record your learning in the log below.

	Creative method	Date tried	What did I like about it?	What was difficult about it?
A	Reverse brainstorming			
B	Curiosity			
C	Multiple uses			
D	Open mind			
E	Random words			
F	Diversify your stimuli			

Exercise 6.5

THINKING THROUGH AN IDEA IN MORE DETAIL

What if you have too many ideas and they never move forwards? If this is your tendency, and your high score on openness to experience means you only stick with an idea until you can think of the next one, try the following exercise, which will help you to think ideas through in more detail.

→ What is good about this idea?

_____

→ Who is likely to benefit?

_____

→ Why would you turn it into reality?

_____

→ What might the downsides be?

_____

→ Has anyone else tried it before, and what happened if they did?

_____

→ What can you take from your previous experience that would help to make this a reality?

_____

→ How passionate are you about doing this on a scale of 1 to 10 (1 = not very, 10 = very)?

1   **2**   **3**   **4**   **5**   **6**   **7**   **8**   **9**   **10**

_____

→ How difficult might it be to implement?

_____

→ Do you want to do it in order to learn, to prove you can do it or to avoid revealing a lack of competence?

_____

→ What are the first three actions you will take to move this forward?

1 _____

2 _____

3 _____

→ Step 2: Ideas into focus

This step in goal setting is about moving on from having a number of random ideas, about things you might like to do or are thinking about, to bringing them into focus so that you can decide on the one or two that you will do.

Case study

Frank loved gardening and had plenty of ideas of what he could grow in his new small plot. He was excited by the concept of having vegetables and summer fruits, as well as flowers and shrubs. What he found difficult was making a decision about precisely what he would grow, and his indecisiveness meant that he almost missed the time for planting his seeds.

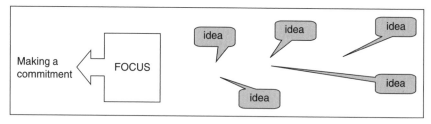

Ideas into focus

This is where the personality trait of neuroticism is highlighted. If an individual has a high score in this dimension of personality, it is likely that they can be sensitive and nervous. Hans Eysenck (see Chapter 2) had a theory that neuroticism is a function of activity in the limbic system – the part of our brain responsible for flight or flight. He suggested that those with a high score for neuroticism are likely to be more often 'on their toes', ready to react to a perceived threat.

Therefore, if someone with a high score in neuroticism has to make a decision about which idea to choose, if there is a perceived threat of the idea not working well enough, a risk of looking stupid or maybe being criticized, then they are likely to put off that activity for as long as possible. If this is your experience, you will be pleased to know that there are several ways in which you can develop a greater tolerance for coping with this type of situation.

COMFORT ZONE

One way to build confidence to take faster decisions is to practise stepping out of your comfort zone. This is the mental boundary that individuals create to give them a feeling of security when operating within an environment where they feel comfortable. For example, if you have always experienced positive results when you have taken quick decisions, it is likely that you feel safe to continue to do this.

However, other people may fear what might happen if they take a quick decision, because of either past experiences or the negative outcome they perceive might happen as a result. In order to encourage someone to step out of their comfort zone and take a risk, it is important that they feel safe enough to be prepared to do so. One way is to have a series of small steps that they can make, and preferably steps in which there are areas of perceived safety or comfort where they can 'recharge' their emotions.

In most cases, the more you practise stepping out of your comfort zone the easier it becomes. In this way you extend your capabilities, your tolerance of discomfort and your ability to take on bigger challenges. The following story highlights ways to expand your comfort zone.

Exercise 6.6

STEPPING OUT OF YOUR COMFORT ZONE

To be able to move from lots of ideas to deciding on one idea, first tell yourself that whatever idea you pick it is the right idea. Then ask yourself the following questions.

➔ What is the worst that can happen if I decide on this idea?

_____

➔ What is an easy first step I can take to make this idea a reality?

_____

Make sure you keep focused on what worked, and only on the idea you have selected.

The following diagram shows how your comfort zone expands as you take small steps to build confidence to take risks.

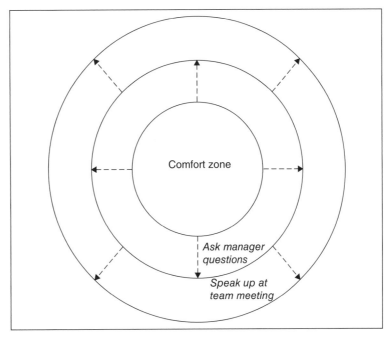

Comfort zone

Ask manager questions

Speak up at team meeting

Expanding your comfort zone

➜ Step 3: Gaining motivation

Once you have decided to narrow down your ideas and commit to one move forwards, the more you can gain motivation to do it the greater the likelihood is that it will happen. If you think about what the word motivation actually means, it's 'motive for action'. So you have to find your motive for action.

Exercise 6.7

In the box below, make a note of the motive for action you have for the different goals in all aspects of your life. As your record builds up, periodically review it and look for trends. Similarly, if there are trends with some of the goals then have a look at the motives.

Is there a common denominator that may be the root cause of the success or the problem?

Exercise 6.8

NOTICE THE LANGUAGE YOU USE

Becoming aware of the language that you use to write down your idea or goal can help to ensure that it motivates you most effectively.

Compare the following pairs of statements and tick the one in each pair that motivates you more.

a. I want to reduce the amount of time I spend in front of the computer each day.		b. I want to improve my ability to communicate with others.	
c. I'd like to lose weight.		d. I want to feel healthier, more energetic and fit into my clothes more comfortably.	
e. I want to avoid being so quiet at business networking functions.		f. I'd like to speak to at least three people I have not met before at the next networking event I attend.	
g. I'd like to reduce the balance on my credit card.		h. I would like to manage my personal finances more effectively.	
i. I want to get away from having to work with my annoying manager.		j. I want to get a job in a different department.	

Review which ones you ticked.

All the goals in the left-hand column (a, c, e, g, i) are written with the 'away from' preference in mind, whereas the ones in the right-hand column (b, d, f, h, j) are a different form of the same goal but written with the 'towards' preference.

'TOWARDS' AND 'AWAY FROM' PREFERENCES

Every one of us will have filtering preferences which guide and direct our motivation and behaviour. Some people are motivated by directing attention towards what they want (pleasure), whereas others prefer to focus on what they want to get away from or avoid (pain).

▶ **Away from** (problem oriented) focuses on getting 'away from' the problem and you may prefer words such as avoid, reduce, get rid of, stop, etc.

▶ **Towards** (goal oriented) is motivated by focusing on the future and what can be achieved, so you may prefer words such as improve, change, gain, better, etc.

It's useful to know your preferences so that you can write your goals in a manner that motivates you. These preferences, also known as meta programs, were originally talked about by neuro-linguistic programming (NLP) gurus Robert Dilts and Judith De Lozier.

AGREEABLENESS AND MOTIVATION

If we view motivation through the lens of the agreeableness trait, it is likely that those with a low score for agreeableness will be motivated to take action because they know that the outcome is likely to benefit them personally. Those at the other end of the scale, however, with a high score for agreeableness, are likely to give everyone else's goals a higher priority than their own. This is because people who score high on this dimension are empathetic, considerate, friendly, generous and helpful. If this is an issue for you, try out the exercise below as it can help you gain motivation for your own goals and priorities, rather than focusing on everyone else's first.

Exercise 6.9

GAINING MOTIVATION

Review what you wrote down for Exercise A in the Introduction, where you identified what you would like to achieve as a result of reading this book.

Question	Answer
How much do you want to achieve it on a scale of 1 to 10 (1 = low, 10 = high)?	If lower than 5, ask yourself what would make it a higher score.
What can I let go of this week, so that I can focus on what I would like to achieve?	
Who else can help me?	
What are the benefits to me of being able to accomplish this?	
What are the benefits to others?	
When I feel guilty about putting myself first, what should I do?	Remember what they say on aeroplanes: put your own oxygen mask on first before putting it on your child. Putting yourself first at times is ok.
How am I likely to feel in a week if I don't make this activity a priority?	

All these questions and your responses should help you gain motivation for taking action and moving your plans forward to the next stage.

→ Step 4: Detailed plan

You may find it easy to identify your goals, be highly motivated to create a plan, and have no trouble coming up with a detailed list of activities and tasks required to make it happen. However, the planning element may end up being constrained because you want the outcome to be 'right' and are not prepared to settle for anything less than perfection (or a close facsimile!). This characteristic can be recognized as a high score for conscientiousness.

By contrast, if you have a low score for conscientiousness you will have a more easy-going approach, where nothing is tied down and flexibility rules. You enjoy the freedom to 'go with the flow' and generally dislike the idea of a detailed plan.

Here are some useful tips for both preferences.

Low conscientiousness: enjoys flexibility and freedom	High conscientiousness: tends to be organized and seeks perfection
Being organized and writing a plan is likely to be something you don't enjoy, but others may need one in order to give them confidence or to be willing to help you.	Preparation and planning enable you to have greater flexibility if things change, so are useful up to a point. But you need to remember the Pareto Principle, or the 80:20 rule.
If your plan is all in your head and not written down, consider whether you can give others some milestones, which will satisfy their need to have some direction but leave you to work out the 'how' of getting there in whatever way suits you.	When is a plan good enough? Ask yourself whether the extra time and effort put into getting something perfect may be outweighed by the lesser amount of time you may have to accomplish the outcome.
Remember (see Chapter 3) that those who write down their goals are more likely to achieve them. It can be as simple as a diagram or a few words on the back of an envelope, but it can help you focus on keeping on track.	Remember that your perception of what is 'right' is just that – your perception. Another person could have a different view. Think of a time when you have been comfortable to 'go with the flow'. What were the factors that enabled you to feel okay about doing so, and how could you replicate that feeling in different areas of your life or work?

SET A GOAL

Right now, just write down a quick outline of one goal that you would like to achieve in the next few months.

Within the next _____ months, I intend to _____

_____

I will know that it is progressing because _____

_____ ,

which will mean that _____

_____

I will take the following action as my first step on the

journey: _____

by _____ and share this action with _____
because I know that they will support and help me achieve
my overall goal.

→ Step 5: Share with others

The final step in this stage of the goal-setting process is to share your goal with others. This can help you build your motivation for achieving the goal by testing your thinking and possibly gaining alternative perspectives or ideas that can improve your goal plan. In addition, you may find that by sharing your goal you gain support from an external source.

The previous steps all relate to working up an idea into a concrete plan, which is likely to be an internally driven process, and it's now time to take your goals to the outside world. This fifth step will be addressed in the next chapter.

What I have learned

REFLECTIONS

What are my thoughts, feelings and insights on what I have read so far?

```



```

YOUR JOURNEY

Summarize any actions you have identified as a result of reading this chapter.

Chapter	Actions
Introduction	
What is personality? 1 Personality: how temperament and character define you 2 Personality assessment tools and tests 3 How to use personality assessments	
Assessing where you are 4 The five dimensions of personality 5 Your personality, goal setting and achievement	
Setting goals 6 How to set goals that will motivate you	

Where to next?

This chapter has outlined how to set goals that will motivate you, by understanding how your personality influences and impacts on the different stages of goal formulation. The next chapter develops the theme of setting goals by putting them into the wider context, helping you to appreciate how external influences can influence and impact on your motivation, focus and direction.

7 Positioning your goals in a wider context

- ▶ *How can I get 'buy-in' for my goal?*
- ▶ *How could my personality influence how others affect my goal?*
- ▶ *What are the external factors that can influence my goal?*
- ▶ *How can I avoid disappointments and surprises when working towards my goal?*

One of the keys to positioning your goal is in your assessment and understanding of the external factors. Another key aspect is the detail with which you think about *how* you will achieve your goal. The quality of work you put into these two factors is what will enable you to be well prepared and able to communicate confidently about your goal.

Without thinking carefully about this final step and considering the possible influencers on the path towards your goal, your likelihood of success is much reduced. You will need to realize that you will do a better job if you have the security of a well-thought-through goal plan, which means involving other people in that plan.

'A goal properly set is halfway reached.'

Abraham Lincoln, US President (1809–65)

→ Your personality and step 5

Your scores for the five personality dimensions will influence your approach to this stage. For example, if you score highly for conscientiousness and enjoy focusing on detail, you will also undoubtedly feel reluctant to share your thoughts with others; if you are a low scorer in this dimension, you may feel confident that you will be able to talk or think your way out of any problems by yourself.

Similarly, people with a high score for extraversion are likely to find talking to others easy. The danger is that, in doing the talking, they are not doing much listening, which is how useful comments can be picked up from others. Those at the other end of the scale, who have a low score for extraversion, may feel reluctant to approach others and will probably prefer to have indirect communication with them, i.e. through email or letter. The danger in this method is that words can be misconstrued and the meaning lost because there is no body language or verbal expression to add colour to what is written.

Exercise 7.1

WHO SHOULD YOU SPEAK TO?

To prepare for the final step of involving others in your goal, you first need to begin to consider the wider context of your goal, which can impact on and influence your journey towards achieving it.

With your goal in mind, answer the following questions.

→ Who are the 'primary people' who will be directly involved in working with you on your goal?

_____

_____

→ What are the tasks the primary people need to perform?

_____

_____

→ What are the external factors that could impact or influence the achievement of your goal?

_____

_____

→ What aspects of the goal do you not look forward to doing?

_____

_____

Now refer back to Exercise 1.6 in Chapter 1 and review your energy (stimulus) preferences, then look again at your answers above to make sure your 'personality preferences' have not tricked you into missing any external factor, people or task. Make corrections to your answers if you need to.

→ Stretching your capabilities

Research (Hollenbeck and Klein, 1987) has found that, when difficult goals are set autonomously (i.e. by you), there is greater goal commitment, which in turn leads to greater performance. Similarly, when people have previously set their own tough goals, they are more likely to achieve higher performance with their future goals, irrespective of whether these goals are autonomous or imposed.

If this point surprises you, it may indicate that your particular combination of conscientiousness, agreeableness and neuroticism means you are less inclined to challenge yourself. Therefore, in considering the support that you may benefit from and that will help stretch your performance, aim to choose someone whom you believe in and trust.

COMPETITION AND SUCCESS

Think about people you know who are eager to 'have a go' and take risks and who always seem happy, regardless of whether things are going well or not. They may have tried something they really wanted to do and were open to celebrating their achievements, great or small. A combination of openness to experience and extraversion will be the dominant traits in these cases, but don't underestimate the part that neuroticism can also play in those who succeed and compete well, as the clues may be more subtle.

When thinking about the idea of competing, don't just think of sport. Competing in this context refers to engaging with your intent and focus to achieve very good results. Therefore a sense of pride may be a context through which you could build a progressive way to stretch yourself more.

We are not always the best judge of our performance; most high performers in business, sport and other walks of life use coaches, mentors and other specialists to help them fine-tune and develop their performance. One benefit of being open-minded to input from a wider context, such as from advisers or supporters, is that we all have habits and we are continually developing and reinforcing them in such a way that they can limit our performance.

These habits can cause us to be lazy, which is not a sin because relaxation is important; however, so is developing and nurturing our abilities, because staying in your comfort zone can become de-energizing.

CONTEMPLATING FAILURE

Another reason for staying in our comfort zone is that we may not want to make a mistake or, worse still, fail. We are therefore reluctant to stretch our 'risk envelope'. However, others can help us believe that we have more capability than we thought and can help us to stretch our performance or to try something different.

Case study

An example of how you can re-evaluate failure is the story of Jessica Ennis, the British track and field athlete specializing in multi events. She was a rising star, but a foot injury meant that she had to miss the 2008 Beijing Olympics, which one might describe as a failure. However, after a 12-month lay-off she returned to competition feeling determined to do even better than before and at the London Olympics in 2012 she won the gold medal in the heptathlon event. Out of a setback, which one might have viewed as a failure at the time, came renewed focus and determination.

Exercise 7.2

REFRAMING FAILURE

Some people describe life as a kaleidoscope of learning opportunities, regarding failure as just something that happens. They will say 'failure is what you make of it'.

What does failure mean to you?

_____

_____

Write down your definition of failure here.

_____

_____

Write down any other words or phrases you might use in place of failure.

_____

_____

_____

_____

_____

Now think about five situations in your life which you regard as failures and enter them in the left-hand column of the table below. In the middle column list the learning you gained from each, and in the third column write down one of the alternative words or phrases you gave above for 'failure' against each learning.

Failure	Learning	Reframe
1		
2		
3		
4		
5		

Finally, review the learning points and consider how else you might have gained that learning. Then consider how – with your goals and other tasks and actions in your life – you could be more optimistic and kinder to yourself in the vocabulary you use to describe events where you do not succeed or when things go wrong.

As you begin to look at your goal in a wider context so you may find you experience a range of sensations, from denial, resistance and reticence to acceptance, commitment and excitement. If you find yourself becoming stuck, think about where you might be on the change curve shown below.

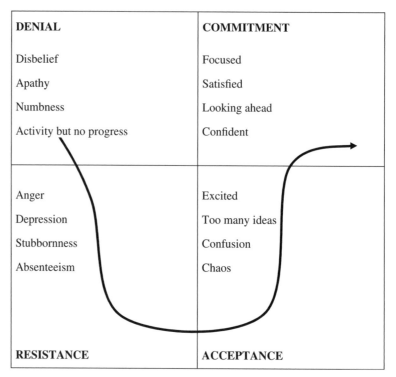

DENIAL	COMMITMENT
Disbelief	Focused
Apathy	Satisfied
Numbness	Looking ahead
Activity but no progress	Confident
Anger	Excited
Depression	Too many ideas
Stubbornness	Confusion
Absenteeism	Chaos
RESISTANCE	ACCEPTANCE

The change curve

→ Trying new experiences

One benefit of trying new experiences, whether they are unusual situations or challenges, is that you can discover new things about yourself. People who tend to be more reactive than proactive may be less inclined to seek out a new stimulus themselves, preferring to wait for new experiences to arrive rather than seeking them out. However, whether a new experience presents itself or you choose it, you will learn how you react, reflect and respond to it. Faced with a new environment, new people or new demands, you will have an opportunity to develop your inner strength, sensitivity and stamina.

Part of the skill in finding new experiences to benefit from is not to be too extreme too early; if our fear takes over, we cannot assimilate the positive experience. The environment in which you tackle a new experience will be a factor here: for example, the less extrovert may not wish to experiment in front of others, or only with those who know them, or they may just want to have one friend for support. On the other hand, someone who is highly extrovert may be enthusiastic and confident to take on a big challenge but, if they lack the counterbalance of, say, conscientiousness, they may not consolidate much learning from the experience.

It's also worth bearing in mind that, with a goal where you have to rely on or engage others, encouraging them and showing your appreciation will make their job all the easier. The role of encouragement can be a good one for a trusted friend as well as a buddy/confidant.

→ Your choice of supporter

Who you choose as your supporter is an interesting question. Do you pick someone with similar personality traits to you, or someone who is quite different and can bring another perspective to your thinking?

Sometimes it may be a matter of your ability to build and enjoy better relationships with others who are different from you. This requires understanding and being adept at managing our own personality as well as recognizing and accommodating other people's personality traits.

One question to consider is how you can anticipate and consider the wider context so that you can create an optimal working relationship with your supporters, rather than one that is less effective or that suffers from 'groupthink' – the mode of thinking that happens when the desire for harmony in a decision-making group overrides a realistic appraisal of alternatives. Group members try to minimize conflict and reach a consensus decision without critically evaluating alternative ideas or viewpoints.

Another interesting observation arose from the research mentioned earlier in the chapter around goal setting. This was a study of salespeople who were asked to rate the level of difficulty of their goals using a four-point scale: nearly impossible or very difficult = 4; moderately difficult = 3; moderately easy = 2; and very easy to achieve = 1. When their supervisors were asked to rate the salesperson's goals, the correlation was close: 70 per cent of the supervisors rated a goal as being nearly impossible or very difficult and no supervisor used the lowest rating of very easy to achieve.

Although you may not want your choice of buddy/confidant to be either a taskmaster or someone who will always agree with what you think, you will want to select someone who will both support and challenge you in a way that heightens your motivation and confidence to achieve the goal. If you have not already done so, it may be time to consider who you might use as a buddy/confidant for those difficult moments with your goal when you want to chat through a problem or a challenge you are facing. Who will that person be?

Your temptation may be to pick someone you are comfortable with, but their personality may be such that they will not challenge or support you sufficiently in the pursuit of your goal. Selecting the right person is often not easy and one of the most important things is that their personality should gel with yours.

In thinking about your two personalities, it's also worth considering the circumstance in which they may not gel well and how you will deal with that. This could be because of a clash of personality traits or because one person does not understand or want to consider the other person's view. Clearly, while too much conflict would be unhealthy, confidence to cope with being challenged can provide a more 'balanced' perspective on the way to achieving your goal(s).

→ Involving others in the plan

In trying to prepare how you might set out your goal 'plan of action' and identify who to discuss it with, you are most likely to start by listing the steps you'll need to take from the present through to the conclusion of the goal. While this will provide a logical approach to how the goal can be achieved, it's useful to bear in mind the following points.

▶ You should seek the wider context by getting the views of others who may be involved.

- ▶ Specific information and knowledge about things that may be new to you may go beyond your current experience and knowledge. (You don't know what you don't know.)

- ▶ The steps you have listed may be over- or understated in terms of the time and resources required.

By engaging in dialogue with those involved in the first two points above, you can check that you have all the right steps placed in the right sequence and a good sense of the time and resources required.

Reverse scheduling is taking a job with a number of tasks and allocating those tasks to resources in reverse order from an end delivery date, and scheduling the tasks on the resources. Using the process of reverse scheduling, you start at the end of the goal and work your way back in time, re-examining each step to ensure that you have the right allowance of time and resource for each step.

As you work your way back and review the tasks to be done, adding in any safety allowance for the unexpected or for delays, difficulties and mistakes, you are likely to find that you will need to adjust your expectation of when or how the goal may be achieved.

It is at this point that it is useful to have a review session with your buddy/confidant, to talk through any alterations to the goal and ideas for adjusting your personal approach in terms of your personality traits.

Exercise 7.3

EXPLAINING YOUR GOAL

Bearing in mind the principles of reverse scheduling as described above, use the box below to prepare an explanation of your goal – what it is, the reason why you've chosen it, how important it is to you and your approach to achieving it.

Now write down in more detail what you want from your buddy/confident and how they can support you. Don't forget to re-iterate how they will benefit from supporting you as well as how their support will benefit you. Use the prompts listed below to consider all the aspects.

→ The importance of the buddy/confidant role, e.g. how you value them and their experience and life story

→ Your openness to feedback, e.g. your respect for their opinions

```
┌─────────────────────────────────────────┐
│                                           │
│                                           │
│                                           │
└─────────────────────────────────────────┘
```

→ Your willingness to make adjustments (based on feedback), e.g. your enthusiasm for learning from new experiences

```
┌─────────────────────────────────────────┐
│                                           │
│                                           │
│                                           │
└─────────────────────────────────────────┘
```

→ What personality traits you will find difficult to deal with, e.g. impatience or intolerance of their steady approach

```
┌─────────────────────────────────────────┐
│                                           │
│                                           │
│                                           │
└─────────────────────────────────────────┘
```

You may also find it useful to revisit Exercise 7.1 and talk through each of your answers with your supporter, and then you can list the outcomes of the discussion. Practise what you want to say; think about how it will come over to them. You don't want a simple 'Yes'; you want an enthusiastic, respectful 'Yes', ideally followed by a declaration of how they can support you.

For example, you could say:

▶ how this goal is going to impact you, i.e. what it means to you at the emotional and intellectual level
▶ what motivates you and demotivates you
▶ what's important to you about the goal and what's unimportant, irrelevant or a distraction
▶ what role, contributions and strengths you are looking for from them.

Use the tables below to summarize your key points.

The goal	
The reason (for the goal)	

Keep things brief at this stage, with no more than five points for the steps and challenges of your goal. You can go into more detail at a later stage. Remember that first impressions can give you a winning advantage.

The five main steps of the goal	The five main challenges you will face
1	1
2	2
3	3
4	4
5	5

Now, fill in this table.

The outcomes	
What it will mean to you	
What your achievement of the goal could mean to them	

Now that you have clarity about the support you want and the type of personality that will and won't suit you, you can begin to draw up a shortlist of people you would like to be your buddy/confidant to work with you on a goal you have. Remember what you are wanting them to do for you, which may include challenging you, so be prepared for possibly feeling some apprehension as you approach them. Once you are ready, pick the right moment to make your request.

Think about the personality of your preferred supporter and what the best way may be for them to receive your request. Although you may want to send an email – perhaps because you're shy and don't want to face them or are worried they may say no and you don't want to face rejection – the best chance of success is to approach them in a way that works *for them*.

With the advantage of a buddy/confidant who can support you, provide counsel, offer different ways of thinking and points of view and challenge you, you will be better placed to consider a much wider context for your goal. At this time you can revisit both the external and the internal factors including conflicting constraints, people and coping strategies.

→ Review and reflection

As you achieve each step towards your goal, take the time to both enjoy the satisfaction of having completed it and reflect on the wider context of what you have learned. Reward yourself appropriately and be sure to recalibrate your self-confidence and your belief in your ability to achieve more.

Consider the following points before undertaking the next exercise.

1 If you achieved your goal too easily, make your next goal harder.

2 If you learned something that you can use to help you in the future, then change the future goals.

3 If you think your own personality traits are inhibiting your enjoyment of life, think of some positive alterations (changes) you could make and carry them out.

4 If your goal took too long or was too demoralizing to achieve, then make the next goal a little bit easier.

5 If you noticed a shortfall or weakness in your skills, consider whether your future goals can help you develop that limitation. If future goals could be hampered by the limitation, you may need to think about extending the goal target time or outcome, or even undertake some learning or training before you start working on your next goal.

Exercise 7.4

REVIEW YOUR GOAL PLANS

Now review the rest of your goal plans. What adjustments do you need to make or would you like to make?

Adjustment	Need to make (✓)	Would like to make (✓)

→ Navigating the wider context successfully

From the personality perspective as well as from the understanding of team dynamics, recognizing other people's preferences, influences and orientations will help you gain a broader insight into what may influencing your own behaviour and the progress of your actions towards your goal or project.

The following diagram shows a typical transition curve which has been overlaid with some of the emotional states people can experience as they progress through a change. In the life of a goal or project it is conceivable that there will be many periods of change or adjustment, so these emotional states may be experienced more than once.

Recognizing or, better still, anticipating the next state on the road to real progress may help you adjust your personality so that you can manage your way through the state. A desire to escape the situation may arise as a result of feelings of fear, denial, threat or anger, possibly leading to depression.

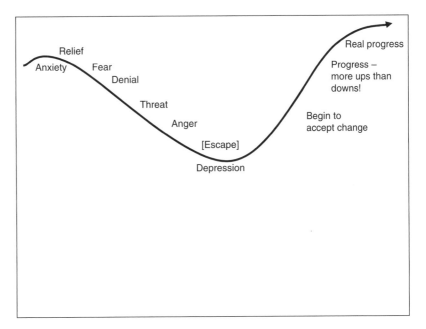

A transition curve

Exercise 7.5

USING THE TRANSITION CURVE

Referring to the transition curve diagram on the previous page, consider a recent goal or project.

→ Against each step of the transition, write down any learning or key observations you experienced during the life of the goal or project which would help ensure that you do a job at least as good next time.

→ Next, mark against any notable steps in the transition where your personality either hindered or helped your progress. (For example, you may have got angry and that had a detrimental effect on your judgement.)

→ Identify an action that would address changes you can make to the habits and behaviours that hindered you.

_____

_____

_____

_____

_____

_____

_____

Finding the right person to help you is not always easy, and it may be helpful to consider whether you need to find more than one supporter to help you at different stages during the lifetime of the activity. For example, someone who is great on strategy and planning at the beginning of the process may not the best person to help you with taking action and maintaining motivation.

What I have learned

REFLECTIONS

What are my thoughts, feelings and insights on what I have read so far?

YOUR JOURNEY

Summarize any actions you have identified as a result of reading this chapter.

Chapter	Actions
Introduction	
What is personality? 1 Personality: how temperament and character define you 2 Personality assessment tools and tests 3 How to use personality assessments	
Assessing where you are 4 The five dimensions of personality 5 Your personality, goal setting and achievement	
Setting goals 6 How to set goals that will motivate you 7 Positioning your goals in a wider context	

Where to next?

This chapter has outlined the importance of positioning your goals in a wider context, so that you benefit from the insight of others and understand how the broader landscape may impact on your aspirations. The next two chapters will guide you through a number of practical steps to help you cope with your 'inner world' and for dealing with other people's personality traits that may impact on you.

8 Managing your inner performance

- ▶ *I tend to get distracted as I begin to work on a goal. How can I stay on track?*
- ▶ *How important is mindset in goal achievement?*
- ▶ *What techniques can I use to maintain a positive attitude towards my goal?*
- ▶ *How do I bounce back from disappointments?*

Why do some organizations that use personality assessments still have high turnover, low morale and engagement issues with employees? Surely, if understanding personality was the answer, they would provide more motivated staff who could achieve higher performance. As an individual, you might think that knowing your personality traits would cause you to achieve your goals. However, there is another factor at play: mindset.

Some people have a fixed mindset in which they believe their personality is fixed and cannot be changed, and they will spend a lot of time proving this point to others. Some people have a different mindset and assume that they can adapt their personality where required in order to achieve what they want. The latter approach is the one described in this chapter, which will address the question of 'inner performance' or mindset, defined as those habitual or characteristic mental attitudes that determine how you interpret and respond to situations.

Exercise 8.1

BELIEFS AND MINDSET

Write down one goal from the previous two chapters that you would like to progress.

_____

Rate how challenging you find this goal on a scale of 1 (not very) to 5 (very).

_____

Circle the box below that would define your preferred way of working. The examples relate to preferences identified by someone who has to raise £1,000 sponsorship for an expedition.

External	People
Enjoy practical activities and being active, e.g. bag packing at supermarket	Enjoy being sociable and around people, e.g. getting a group of friends to arrange a fundraising skydive with me
Internal	Task
Enjoy working on own, self-reflection, individual, e.g. writing emails to potential sponsors	Enjoy data and doing things, e.g. researching good fundraising ideas

Now think about the mindset you may have to adopt in order to be successful with your goal. Is this mindset different from your normal mental attitude?

_____

_____

What would you have to believe about yourself, in order to behave in a way that is not your preferred style?

_____

_____

_____

_____

→ Behaviour and mindset

Beliefs are fundamental to managing our mindset because they will drive our behaviour, which ultimately delivers the outcome, as shown in the following diagram.

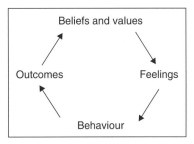

Managing mindset

For example, if you normally enjoy working on your own, and the goal you have set yourself will involve being part of a team, it means you may have to acknowledge that it will be worth while because it will be easier, quicker and maybe even more enjoyable. That type of belief is therefore more likely to generate a positive behaviour in relation to others.

It is useful to understand where beliefs fit into a wider model of change, so that when you encounter an obstacle in working towards your goal, you can pinpoint where the resistance is likely to be.

Case study

Vince decided that he wanted to write a book and to complete it within six months. When he got home every night after work, he sat down at his computer and tried to begin. But he found it was not the right place for this as there were too many distractions, so he decided to change the environment and go to the library. After a couple of weeks, he realized that he needed to be disciplined, and decided to write three nights a week for a couple of hours. But progress was slow.

Vince then spoke to a friend, who suggested that he should go on a writing course to learn how to do it properly. Vince took the advice and enrolled and, having paid out a fair amount of cash for a weekend course, felt more confident when he next sat down in front of the computer. But his progress was still slow. Why? What was really stopping him?

Try as he might, he could not see himself as a writer, and so every time he sat down to write his subconscious mindset was 'I don't believe I can write an entire book.' Having eventually realized this, Vince decided to change his mindset to 'I am a writer' and just start writing about anything. Once he got into a regime of an hour's writing every evening on any subject, it gave him the confidence to start writing the book, and within three months he had completed it.

THE LOGICAL LEVELS

The logical levels model grew out of work by Gregory Bateson and found a home in neuro-linguistic programming (NLP). NLP pioneer Robert Dilts is often credited for popularizing it. The diagram below shows these 'logical levels of change', and they give a clue about why the levels that Vince tried to change – the environment and then his skills – did not work because the level at which he had his writer's block was at the belief level.

Each logical level in the hierarchy organizes the information below it. So if you change something on a lower level (such as your environment), it will not necessarily affect the levels above it. However, making a change at a higher level – beliefs in Vince's case – will change everything below it.

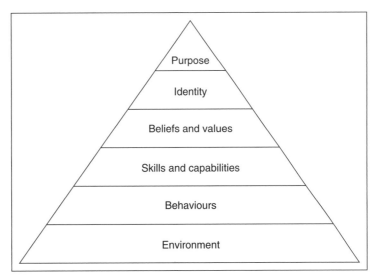

The logical levels of change

Exercise 8.2

USING THE LOGICAL LEVELS

Having read about the logical levels of change model and the case study, review the goal that you want to achieve and identify any levels at which there may be blockages or obstacles. Start with the Environment level and work up to Purpose.

→ My goal: _____

The logical levels

→ **Environment:** is environment an issue?

_____

→ **Behaviours:** what behaviour is required?

_____

_____

→ **Skills and capabilities:** are skills important to this goal?

_____

→ **Beliefs:** what beliefs or values do you hold that may get in the way of you achieving this goal?

_____

→ **Identity:** how does this goal relate to your identity?

_____

_____

→ **Purpose:** does your goal fit in with your overall purpose (as a human being)?

_____

Obstacles

→ If there is an obstacle to moving forward, which level is it at?

_____

→ What actions could you take to overcome this obstacle?

_____

→ What will you do?

_____

....

The story of Vince shows that he had set himself a goal but did not truly believe it was possible to achieve. By becoming more aware of what was really going on and being prepared to face up to the situation, he was able to take a different approach, which delivered the result he wanted.

Many organizations typically invest a lot of money in training courses (skills and capabilities level) and are then perplexed to discover that, when the employees go back to work, they still don't deliver the performance required. That's because the issue is generally not about skills but higher up the model (beliefs and values, identity or purpose level). These are the issues that are difficult to spot, as it's only the result of that 'inner performance' (i.e. the behaviour) that others can observe. So they try to fix the symptom and not the underlying cause.

Exercise 8.3

LEARNING FROM SUCCESS

It is also possible to use the logical levels model to learn from your previous success in goal setting and achievement, in order to be able to replicate that success in other situations.

Identify a goal that you successfully achieved either at work or in your personal life, and then answer the following questions, where 1 = low and 5 = high.

→ To what degree did the goal relate to your wider aims in life (your purpose)?

1   2   3   4   5

→ How important was having a clear sense of your brand or identity to the success?

1   2   3   4   5

→ Make a list of the values (such as excellence, integrity) that supported you or helped you achieve your goal.

_____

_____

_____

→ How important to your success were having and communicating those values to others?

1   2   3   4   5

→ How important to your success was 'believing in' what you were doing?

1   2   3   4   5

→ List the beliefs that supported or motivated you to follow through and succeed.

_____

_____

→ List the specific skills and capabilities that contributed to your success.

_____

_____

→ How important to your success was having specific skills and capabilities?

1   2   3   4   5

→ What specific behaviours and actions were responsible for your success?

_____

_____

→ To what degree did environment play a part in the success of the goal?

1   2   3   4   5

Now review your answers for each of the logical levels and reflect on which aspect(s) seem to be most important for you to remember in future.

_____

_____

_____

How can you apply this learning when tackling future goals?

_____

_____

→ Modelling

You have now reviewed a success in one area of your life or work and applied the learning from that situation to address your current area of focus. This concept, called 'modelling', can also be used to observe and replicate the behaviour, language and beliefs of another person in order to get the same behavioural outcome as they do.

If you observed someone who was excellent at networking and always seemed friendly, talked to lots of other people and enjoyed themselves, you could watch what they do, but what is difficult is to unpick what their mindset is that enables them to behave in that particular manner.

Using the modelling process can help you understand the aspects of another person's personality and how their attitude and mindset impact on their behaviour.

Exercise 8.4

THE MODELLING PROCESS

Use the following questions to interview someone you know who sets and achieves goals successfully. Their answers can give you a clue to their mindset, and then you can choose whether to adopt any of their strategies for yourself.

Before you begin, set their expectations by explaining the process you'll follow: 'I want to learn from you about your ability to set and achieve goals successfully. My job is to ask questions about the patterns of your experience that enable you to do this really well.'

→ Please explain the context in which you normally set and achieve goals successfully, for example at work.

→ Using a recent example of when you set and achieved a challenging goal, how did you organize and manage your environment?

→ What are you thinking about or saying to yourself as you are progressing?

→ What effect does your behaviour have on the outcomes you achieve?

→ How do you do what you do (e.g. set the outcome, focus on it, overcome obstacles, etc.)?

_____

→ What is important to you when you focus on achieving a goal?

_____

→ What do you use as evidence to know that you are accomplishing your objective? What do you see, hear or feel?

_____

→ What do you do to get this goal or outcome? Can you describe specific steps and actions that you use to achieve your stated goal?

_____

→ What values are important to you when you are focused on your goal? What beliefs enable you to do this activity really well?

_____

→ What do you do if things go wrong? Is there a plan B? What would someone notice about you?

_____

→ What makes it possible for you to be goal-oriented?

_____

→ What motivates you to set and achieve challenging goals?

_____

→ Neuroticism and inner performance

One of the characteristics of people who tend to score high on neuroticism is their level of emotional response to events that would not affect most people. They may find it difficult to think clearly when coping with stress. If something threatens to throw them off course when they are setting or working towards a challenging goal, understanding how they are thinking can be extremely helpful.

An individual's attributional style is the key to understanding why people respond differently to adverse events. American psychologist Martin Seligman's work developed the theory of learned helplessness, from which further research, including Bernard Weiner's attribution theory, was concerned with the way that people attribute a cause or explanation to an unpleasant event such as a problem when working in pursuit of a goal.

ATTRIBUTIONAL THINKING

When a good or bad situation occurs, we attribute the outcome to three different factors:

1 **Time**

   permanent – 'It always happens.'

   temporary – 'It occasionally happens.'

2 **Personal**

   internal – 'I caused it to happen.'

   external – 'Someone or something else caused it.'

3 **Universal**

   global – 'It happens everywhere.'

   specific – 'It happens in specific situations.'

Over time, individuals build up a pattern of thinking related to these three factors.

Individuals with high scores on neuroticism and low scores on extraversion may consistently attribute negative events to sources that are permanent (it always happens), internal (I caused it to happen) and global (it happens everywhere). In other words, if something bad happens, an individual will typically think that problems like this always happen, it's their fault and it's never going to change in similar situations in future.

By contrast, individuals who exhibit a more positive explanatory style attribute their failures to causes that are temporary (it sometimes happens), external (something else caused it outside my control) and specific (it was a one-time event). That way, they can more quickly bounce back from disappointment or overcome obstacles because of how they attribute the events in their mind.

It can be challenging to help individuals flip around their attributional style, but it's not impossible. Like all changes, the first step towards this shift is increased awareness. Our attributional thinking style determines our ability to be resilient, enterprising and cope with challenges that we may face in working towards our goals or adapting our personality style to help us get the results we want. It also determines our behaviour, which is in response to that thinking.

Exercise 8.5

Think about how you respond to different situations, when you are trying to adapt your personality, using these three steps:

- ▶ A situation occurs.
- ▶ You form a thought or belief about the situation.
- ▶ You take action (behave) in response to that thought or belief.

For example, if a friend passes you in the street and doesn't acknowledge you, you may think either (a) 'What's up with her?' or (b) 'I must have done something to upset her.'

As a result, you either (a) ask her what the matter is or (b) avoid her in future and feel upset.

Circle either a or b in both steps to show which thought you would have and the action you would take.

Write down a summary of a recent situation where you responded in a way that was not helpful.

What did you say to yourself about that event? Circle the choices below.

Time

▶ permanent – 'It always happens.'

▶ temporary – 'It occasionally happens.'

Personal

▶ internal – 'I caused it to happen.'

▶ external – 'Someone or something else caused it.'

Universal

▶ global – 'It happens everywhere.'

▶ specific – 'It happens in specific situations.'

If you had a chance to revisit that event and think about it differently, how else could you view it?

_____

_____

In order to become aware of how you attribute events and situations that happen to you, it's a good idea to keep a diary with headings as in the following example, which gives sample entries for one day.

Diary record			
Day	Events	How was I thinking?	What will I do differently?
Monday	I went to a networking meeting and felt nervous. I stood at the buffet and not many people spoke to me.	This always happens. I caused it to happen. It happens in specific situations.	I realize it will keep happening unless I change my mindset. I want to enjoy these events and aim to meet one interesting person.
Tuesday			
Wednesday			
Thursday			
Friday			
Saturday			
Sunday			

→ Risk is what you make of it

Another significant aspect of managing your inner performance is risk. Risk is all around us so you can try to minimize it, avoid it, ignore it or embrace it, but probably the best approach is that you manage it. To manage risk you'll need to understand your propensity for, tolerance of and attitude towards risk. There are various development assessment tools you can use, including Geoff Trickey's Risk-Type Compass®, shown here.

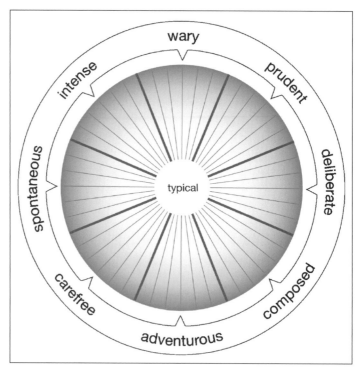

The Risk-Type Compass®

PCL's validated research into risk led to eight distinct risk types being used to define an individual's response to risk taking and ability to manage risk. These eight types are drawn from four of the five dimensions of personality: extraversion, conscientiousness, neuroticism and openness to experience. The fifth dimension – agreeableness – was not included in the Risk-Type Compass® as there was insufficient consistency of research data available.

These are the eight risk types:

▶ **Wary**
Very low risk tolerance. Anxious, self-disciplined and cautious, they try to eliminate risk and uncertainty. Fearful that things are bound to go wrong, they seek to control everything.

▶ **Prudent**
Low risk tolerance. Self-controlled and detailed in their planning, this type is organized and systematic. Conforming and conventional, they are most comfortable with continuity and familiarity.

▶ **Deliberate**
Average risk tolerance. Systematic and compliant, they tend to be calm, optimistic and self-confident. They experience little anxiety but never walk into anything unprepared.

▶ **Composed**
High risk tolerance. The composed type is cool-headed and optimistic. Seemingly almost oblivious to risk, they take everything in their stride and bounce back from disaster.

▶ **Adventurous**
Very high risk tolerance. The adventurous type is both impulsive and fearless. They combine a deep constitutional calmness with an impulsivity and a willingness to challenge convention.

▶ **Carefree**
High risk tolerance. Spontaneous and unconventional, they are daring, excitement seeking and sometimes reckless. Their impatience and imprudence make life exciting.

▶ **Spontaneous**
Average risk tolerance. Uninhibited and excitable, they enjoy spontaneity but are distraught when things go wrong. Passion and imprudence make them exciting but unpredictable.

▶ **Intense**
Low risk tolerance. Highly strung, pessimistic and self-critical, they take things personally and feel defeated when things go wrong.

There are two major influences on our propensity for risk-taking and both are deeply rooted in our personality. Firstly, there is the extent to which we are anxious about our physical or emotional security (whether the plane will crash or affections not be reciprocated). Secondly, we vary in our need for structure, predictability and avoidance of ambiguity (whether the rules and the future are clear and everything is planned and well organized).

These two themes provide the two axes underpinning the Risk-Type Compass. Everybody falls somewhere along both axes, which relate to:

▶ fear of danger or threat to physical or emotional security

▶ the need for structure, clarity, predictability and concern about ambiguity.

The Risk-Type Compass identifies four 'pure' types and four 'complex' types. An individual may be towards one end of the scale of pure types or in the middle (known as 'typical'), depending on their level of risk tolerance.

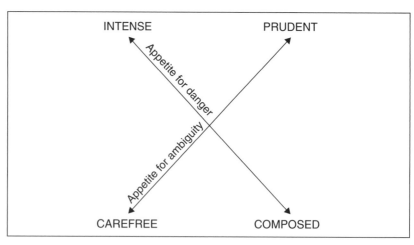

The four pure risk types (Geoff Trickey Psychological Consultancy Ltd)

The remaining four risk types of wary, deliberate, adventurous and spontaneous are regarded as 'complex' risk types as they can combine aspects of their neighbouring types. For example, wary will draw characteristics of intense and prudent, as shown in the following diagram.

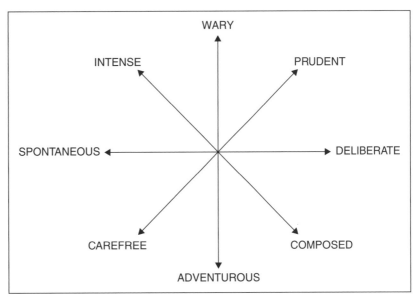

The four complex risk types (Geoff Trickey Psychological Consultancy Ltd)

Risk types and dimensions of personality	
Dimension	Relevance to risk type
Extraversion	High scores are likely to be associated with higher risk tolerance because extraverts need stimulation.
Neuroticism	High scores tend to be related to lower risk tolerance as they tend to focus on fear of failure.
Conscientiousness	High scores tend to be more cautious, compliant and careful and therefore have lower risk tolerance.
Agreeableness	This factor is the least predictive area for risk.
Openness to experience	High scores are more likely to have high risk tolerance because they are tolerant of uncertainty and change.

Exercise 8.6

WHAT'S YOUR RISK TYPE?

Consider the eight risk types described above and your scores on the five dimensions of personality. Write down which risk type you think best describes you.

_____

When you have identified what you think is your risk type, consider the neighbouring types (i.e. those on both sides of your type) and how they may influence you as you work towards your goal.

For example, if you are a carefree risk type, the neighbouring types are adventurous and spontaneous, so you may at times be drawn towards doing things that are adventurous but not perhaps best for your goal. Similarly, you may be drawn to being spontaneous, which could mean that you don't adequately consider its effect on your goal.

Risk type operates at the level of personality and is likely to have an all-encompassing influence. However, propensity for risk is also affected by attitudes, which are nearer the surface and more variable. Attitudes are formed as a result of experience, the climate of opinion, cultural influences and personal circumstances. This accounts for the fact that people will often display different appetites for risk in different risk domains (finance, recreation, social or health and safety risks, for example). However, under stress or pressure they tend to revert to their risk type.

YOUR ATTITUDE TO RISK

Consider a scenario that you have been in or are concerned may occur when working towards a goal that is likely to have risk associated with it.

How does the risk type compass give you insight into how to manage that situation?

_____

_____

Understanding your attitude to risk and the different approaches that others may take can enable you to have greater choice in how you behave in future.

HOW TO STOP WORRYING

For some people, the idea of risk can be worrying, because they fear for the possible consequences of their actions. For example, are they buying the best car for them, or taking the right job? Worrying can mean that they spend a lot of time thinking about bad things and being preoccupied with negative possibilities. So it's important not to let it dominate your thoughts.

Here are some ways to stop yourself worrying.

▶ **Confront your fears.** Sometimes it's the unknown that is worrying, so being able to face up to your fears and identify who can help you, or who you can talk the issue through with, can reduce your concerns.

▶ **With real worries, take real (practical) steps to change things.** Take a good hard look at the situations you can control and those you can't, and work to change those you can control. You can change your mood by changing your thoughts, and doing so one step at a time often works best.

▶ **Do not worry about worrying.** There are reasons both to worry and not to worry. If your reasons to worry are genuinely related to what's happening in your life, don't unnecessarily burden your existing feelings with guilt or other (extraneous) negative feelings.

What I have learned

REFLECTIONS

What are my thoughts, feelings and insights on what I have read so far?

```
┌─────────────────────────────────────────┐
│                                           │
│                                           │
│                                           │
│                                           │
│                                           │
└─────────────────────────────────────────┘
```

YOUR JOURNEY

Summarize any actions you have identified as a result of reading this chapter.

Chapter	Actions
Introduction	
What is personality? 1 Personality: how temperament and character define you 2 Personality assessment tools and tests 3 How to use personality assessments	
Assessing where you are 4 The five dimensions of personality 5 Your personality, goal setting and achievement	
Setting goals 6 How to set goals that will motivate you 7 Positioning your goals in a wider context	
Taking practical steps to improve 8 Managing your inner performance	

Where to next?

This chapter has outlined the importance of understanding and managing your inner performance: this comprises the habitual or characteristic mental attitudes that determine how you will interpret and respond to situations. Now that you have learned in this and the previous chapter about the practical steps you can take to improve, the next steps are to monitor progress and learn the techniques to maintain focus and overcome resistance that suit your personality preference.

9 Navigating others' personality traits

▶ What are the personality traits to look out for when working with others?

▶ How can I cope better with people who are different from me?

▶ What aspects of my personality most often cause relationship problems between me and others?

▶ Why don't I always anticipate how others will perceive me?

The emphasis of this chapter is on navigating – not on changing, altering or persuading people to your way. Depending on how you handle yourself, people's response to you may be positive or negative so, by working well with others, you may be able to influence how they respond to you. It is worth being optimistic when you are dealing with personalities you find difficult because personality traits are malleable, so over time things may become easier because you both adjust.

To navigate well, it is important to know your subject, be highly vigilant, understand what you are recognizing and be responsive when necessary.

'Different people bring out different aspects of one's personality.'

Trevor Dunn, musician (b. 1968)

→ Recognizing and appreciating traits

The following table shows the easily recognizable characteristics of the Big Five personality dimensions described in Chapter 4.

Characteristics of the five dimensions of personality		
Personality dimension	*High/low score*	*Characteristic*
Extraversion	Hi	Energetic, may over-communicate
	Lo	Prefers to think things through before speaking, reflective
Neuroticism	Hi	More likely to interpret ordinary situations as threatening and minor frustrations as difficult
	Lo	Emotionally stable, less reactive to stress
Conscientiousness	Hi	Can over-challenge themselves, highly diligent
	Lo	May break rules, likely not always to complete tasks
Agreeableness	Hi	Compliant, easy to get on with, confident
	Lo	May be cold and distant and seen as aloof
Openness to experience	Hi	Optimistic, has wide range of interests, imaginative
	Lo	Conventional, values tradition, prefers familiar routines

While it's important to remember that an individual's personality is a combination of elements of all these traits, the table provides a rudimentary indicator. It is useful to be able to recognize these traits in others, and how their thinking and behaviour are affected by their traits.

For example, someone who combines a high score in both neuroticism and extraversion can experience an emotional rollercoaster, so what others observe can be confusing and disarming. Where their neuroticism dimension is high, people are likely to be sensitive to environmental stress, perceiving everyday, run-of-the-mill situations as menacing. Problems that linger may lead them to a higher sense of despair. The extraversion trait will encourage some people (those with a high score) to share their emotions and concerns with others, whereas those who have a low score might just avoid communicating because they are thinking about the issue internally and feel less inclined to talk to other people about it.

Case study

David was a first-line manager in a call centre, where daily pressure to maintain call answering levels and deliver customer satisfaction never stopped. His colleagues found him quite draining because he always seemed to be stressed about something or other. If you asked him 'How are you?', you would expect to have at least a five-minute conversation with him, where he retold you his worries of the day so far, such as how the bus was late which meant there were no seats because more people were at the bus stop, and how he was worried that there was unlikely to be an upturn in the economy any time soon.

It seemed that he had developed a habit of making a mountain out of a molehill. This resulted in some of his colleagues purposely avoiding him in the canteen at lunchtime.

Exercise 9.1

If you are looking for someone to work with to help you achieve one of your goals, which requires delivering a project by a specified date in the near future, what would be the traits of the person that you would ideally like to work with, and why?

→ Trait 1

Reason _____

_____

_____

→ Trait 2

Reason _____

_____

_____

→ Trait 3

Reason _____

_____

_____

Example

Trait: Conscientiousness

Reason: High conscientiousness means that the person is likely to be good at planning, being organized, purposeful, achievement oriented and hardworking, with high expectations of themselves. So they will help me stick to the deadline and have a plan to achieve it. The downside is that they may be rigid and uncomfortable if we veer off the agreed plan for any reason.

Another aspect to bear in mind when navigating other people's personality traits is motivation. Motivation is derived from three behaviours, which are:

▶ the choice to expend effort

▶ the choice of level of effort to expend

▶ the choice to persist in that level of effort.

In trying to motivate others, you should therefore consider what the traits are that will drive that individual to employ behaviours in the way that you want. (Go back to the table above to review characteristics of the five dimensions of personality.) You may gain more clues if you refer back to Chapter 1 and consider where people get their energy from (internal, external, people or task) and revisit your notes from Exercise 1.6.

There may be a temptation, when considering your goals and who is involved, to think two-dimensionally – for example, action/skills or culture/behaviour – and forget about the resource required at a particular time. With personality traits it's worth keeping in mind how people are likely to behave over time, particularly if your goal or project is going to take a long while, as some people will lose focus, interest, belief or energy, or get distracted.

Therefore when planning the journey ahead, think about how others are likely to be energized throughout the project, and at what stages they can have a legitimate 'rest stop' in an analogous sense. Think of it as if you were going on a long walk or car journey, and where you will have a rest or comfort break, when you will eat or who will share the driving. In terms of goal planning, try the following exercise.

Exercise 9.2

ANALYSING YOUR TEAM'S TRAITS

On a scale of 1 to 10, what is the level of commitment from each member of your team for each stage of the journey (where 1 = low and 10 = high)?

➔ Team member 1

_____

➔ Team member 2

_____

➔ Team member 3

_____

➔ Others

_____

What are the new things each team member is likely to experience?

➔ Team member 1

_____

➔ Team member 2

_____

→ Team member 3

_____

→ Others

_____

What are the critical goal variables (a variable is something which can cause the project to fail if undetected)?

_____

_____

What are the likely goal difficulties?

_____

_____

What options do you have to get around these difficulties?

_____

_____

What are the personality characteristics of each team member in terms of the Big Five dimensions? In the table below, write your perception of whether they have a high or low score in each area.

Personality dimension	Team member 1	Team member 2	Team member 3	Team member 4	Team member 5	Team member 6
Extraversion						
Neuroticism						
Conscientiousness						
Agreeableness						
Openness to experience						

Reviewing the table, where do you perceive that there may be difficulties in working with a team member on the project or goal?

_____

What will you need to do in order to create an effective working relationship with that person?

_____

Exercise 9.3

HANDLING CRITICISM

As you navigate around other people's personality traits, don't forget how you are thinking, reacting and responding, both internally and externally. For example, while you might be quite happy to get feedback from others and view it as a way to keep improving, others may respond badly to criticism because it reinforces their poor self-perception. This exercise examines how you might handle criticism from others.

Read the statements below, and to the left of each statement put +, 0 or –, according to how you feel you handle it:

+ if you feel you handle the situation well/assertively

0 where you avoid dealing with it

– where you don't handle it well.

1 _____ A peer or friend criticizes you for something you know is not true.

2 _____ Someone (at work) puts you down in a roundabout way (by implication or indirectly) and there is little or no truth in the comment.

3 _____ Your manager criticizes you for a mistake you believe you haven't made and would deny publicly.

4 _____ Someone you respect points out publicly a mistake you have made and you know you have made it (and would agree with it publicly).

5 _____ Someone tells you that your opinion or point of view is stupid.

6 _____ Your manager criticizes you for something you know is not true.

7 _____ Someone criticizes you for a fault you have and would not deny.

8 _____ Things have not been going well for you so your confidence is low and your manager takes you to task for being lax.

Now reflect on your responses and, for each statement, think of someone you know who would respond in the appropriate way to these situations. (who might be a different person for each situation).

1 _____

2 _____

3 _____

4 _____

5 _____

6 _____

7 _____

8 _____

Adapted behaviour

Write down in the table below how you might like to alter your behaviour if you were to face each situation again. State what you think the reaction of the person who made the statement would be, in the light of your changed approach.

Statement	Your adapted personal behaviour	Reaction of the person who made the statement
1		
2		
3		
4		
5		
6		
7		
8		

Now that you have completed this exercise, here are some general guidelines on handling criticism effectively. As you read them, try to think about how you would act both as the receiver of criticism and as the person delivering it.

Guidelines for handling criticism

▶ It's okay to dislike your behaviour and still like yourself.

▶ Deal with the issue first and then your personality.

▶ Separate yourself from criticism; you are not your mistakes.

▶ Modify/improve your behaviour rather than label it or become engaged in judging it.

▶ You are responsible for your behaviours and feelings. They are not other people's responsibility.

→ Types of criticism

In trying to deal with criticism, particularly when it comes from someone who has a different personality from you, it may be useful to consider it in one of these categories:

▶ **Clumsy:** a criticism with some truth in it, delivered inappropriately.

Your response – do not deny, become defensive or attack.

▶ **Unjustified:** a criticism that is untrue.

Your response – be measured, listen and think carefully about it.

▶ **Correct:** a criticism that is valid and delivered in a balanced, appropriate way.

Your response – admit your error and move on.

RESPONDING TO A STIMULUS

By now you will be beginning to see the need to think clearly when navigating and responding to the stimuli around you. To do this well requires a good level of critical thinking, which can be defined as reasonable reflective thinking focused on deciding what to believe or do. Although the word 'critical' is sometimes used in a negative sense, this concept of critical thinking is not negative.

If you have a high score in extraversion, you may find this difficult because you are likely to prefer talking things through than internal thinking. If you are energized by people as opposed to tasks, you may also find it hard because of your preference for the emotional as opposed to the logical facets of a situation.

For example, a manager who thrives on a hands-on, direct, get-it-done, task-driven, energetic approach may not spend the time engaging their 'thinking brain' before driving for action. As a result, they may react to external stimulus in a manner that is ineffective because they have not stopped to question, challenge, ask or consider what they are being told, or have heard, from a third party.

To engage in the process of critical thinking, you will need to draw on the qualities of curiosity, research, active listening, objectivity, humility and creativity. You can achieve this through the behaviours outlined below.

▶ **Curiosity:** having an interest in how things work or happen

▶ **Research:** this means more than simply listening to what is said but engaging in the conversation by asking questions in response

- **Objectivity:** being able to control your emotions in order not to distort judgement, i.e. staying calm and focused

- **Humility:** the ability to not let your ego overrule an idea or plan that is better than yours – you do not know everything

- **Creativity:** stretching yourself, inviting other stimulus, ideas and thoughts

Thinking is not easy for everyone, and critical thinking is even harder. Nevertheless, it is possible, as the characteristics above show. You may have a sense of dread and see critical thinking as a barrier, or you may do it easily and find it hard to understand why others have problems. The next exercise is a critical thinking process that will take you through a series of questions to help you begin to appreciate the skills and attitudes required.

Exercise 9.4

THE CRITICAL THINKING PROCESS

Pick a familiar situation that involved someone with different personality traits from yours. It can be a situation that went well or badly. Next, with the situation uppermost in your mind, go through the following FRISCO process as described by Robert Ennis (2011).

F for Focus
Step into the shoes of the other person(s) involved, and identify their position, arguments and conclusions.

R for Reasons
Identify and evaluate the evidence (what was said or done).

I for Inference
Weigh up the arguments used and the evidence, and see if you can establish the same conclusion, given any alternatives.

S for Situation
Pay close attention to the situation in order to 'read between the lines'.

C for Clarity
Make sure that the meanings were clear and seek clarity if not.

O for Overview
Review the entire process you have gone through, draw your own conclusion and present your point of view.

→ Rivalry and feuds

In some situations, individuals may find it extremely hard to get on with another person. This can be because of rivalry, for example in the sports environment where two competitors have highly focused energy and a desire to achieve the same goal, e.g. a gold medal, and don't wish to contemplate being the one who loses. Away from sport, other examples of rivalry might be two people vying for the charms of the same individual or two employees who both want the top job.

The temperamental character of some individuals may mean that they are impatient, lose their temper and make judgements about others quickly. Feuds begin when one party (correctly or incorrectly) perceives itself to have been attacked, insulted or wronged by another. These feelings of resentment then cause some type of retaliation, which provokes a response from the other person, which then develops into a continual cycle of provocation and retaliation, making it extremely difficult to end the feud.

Feuds can arise in many different circumstances. In football, for example, Sir Alex Ferguson's style and personality mean that he is never far away from conflict, and he has had some high-profile feuds with other people over the years, including David Beckham. Family feuds can also develop, for example when surviving family members attempt to settle the family's estate on the death of a parent or relative, and one party takes action that the other party misinterprets. To settle the matter, lawyers may have to be involved, but this does not necessarily end the feud.

GETTING ON WITH YOUR RIVALS

It may seem like an impossible task to be able to get on with people who view you as a rival, but the answer lies in dealing with the emotional aspects of your personality and realizing that it is possible to turn that rival into a collaborator or ally.

Invariably, as rivalries or feuds develop, trust is reduced. Given that trust is based on reason as well as emotion, the sense of threat worsens often exponentially as the heightened sense of threat leads to a distortion of reason. As negative emotion builds (often based on fear/threat), the hypothalamus – in close association with the limbic system of the brain – sends chemicals like adrenalin, noradrenalin and cortisol into the bloodstream, to get our limbs and muscles ready for running or fighting. Consequently, our rational mind is disengaged, reducing our ability to take in and consider new information.

In other words, as feuds become more intense and rivals more unreasonable, logic and alternative solutions are not well received. To present a solution to a rival or other party in a feud that will be successfully received, the rational side of the brain needs to be engaged, which means addressing the emotional 'hijack' first.

Exercise 9.5

DEALING WITH RIVALRY

Consider a situation either that you are currently facing or that you have been in before, where you have had a feud or rivalry with someone. Work through the following three-stage process to discover how you can adapt your behaviour to get a positive outcome.

1 Re-orientating

Meet on neutral ground, e.g. somewhere like a favourite coffee shop, and through discussion find a way to direct your rival's negative emotions away from you.

> Jeff and Brian both applied for the top job at work, and Jeff was successful. Brian has been Jeff's rival for years, as they are both dynamic, driven and focused on career success. Jeff was delighted with his achievement, but realized that, because he still had to work with Brian, it was best to get his rival onside.

Next, assure your rival that you want to work with them and then reinforce this intention with a discussion about things that you can jointly work on, or have a common interest in. Recognize that the other party is likely to feel angry or hurt, so you may have to listen and let them rant, without reacting, so that they get it 'off their chest'. Try to empathize and imagine how you would have felt if the result had been different. Complete this stage with a positive conversation for both sides.

2 Recognizing

The next step is to 'donate' – give your rival something they want – which may be challenging. This stage is vital, though, so you need to maintain self-control and not to think of asking for something in return; it is purely about giving. (Look back at Exercise 4.7 to see how you scored in relation to being competitive or co-operative.)

> **Jeff decided that he would invite Brian to lead a special project that was coming up, which would give him an opportunity to demonstrate his capabilities and be another achievement to put on his CV. Jeff knew it was a risk because, if Brian failed, it could have a detrimental impact on both their careers.**

It is important to give careful thought to what you would donate. Ideally, it should be something that your rival will want and that will be easy for them to accept. Your aim is that it will be accepted as a genuine and valued gesture. If during this stage you agree to undertake any actions, make sure you deliver them on time and in full.

3 Re-establishing

In this final stage, a new, better relationship should be starting to develop. If your earlier work has gone well, there should be a genuine intention to start trusting each other and working together for each other.

Now is the time to put forward a way of working and, importantly, to seek agreement for it. Use the positive energy of the meeting or discussion to agree on a way forward so that you can both leave highly motivated. As with the previous stage, it's imperative that you deliver your agreed actions on time, so that the other party's positive emotions can be strengthened. It will take time to understand their personality traits and how they may work in a different way from you, so don't be too impatient to see results.

> **Jeff explained to Brian that he recognized his talents and that they could make it a win–win by agreeing to work together for the benefit of both of them.**

What have you learned about getting on with people whom you viewed as rivals?

_____

_____

→ Valuing difference constructively

From what has been discussed so far, you will realize that, when you are working with people who are different from you, you need to be able to step into their view of the world rather than sticking to your own perceptions and filters. With this understanding, you'll be able to treat others in the way they prefer to be treated rather than mistakenly assuming that they will appreciate your style and approach.

For example, just because you may be uncomfortable with conflict does not mean that others are. Some people thrive on disagreement and debate, and it's your ability to be able to value that difference and adapt your style appropriately that will transform your interaction with others.

Opposing temperaments can complement one another and, while it can seem hard at first to work with someone who is diametrically opposed to you, it is possible for you both to be highly effective together.

> **Thought**
>
> Remember to stop and think then react, not react, stop and and then think!

What I have learned

REFLECTIONS

What are my thoughts, feelings and insights on what I have read so far?

> (blank box)

YOUR JOURNEY

Summarize any actions you have identified as a result of reading this chapter.

Chapter	Actions
Introduction	
What is personality? 1 Personality: how temperament and character define you 2 Personality assessment tools and tests 3 How to use personality assessments	
Assessing where you are 4 The five dimensions of personality 5 Your personality, goal setting and achievement	
Setting goals 6 How to set goals that will motivate you 7 Positioning your goals in a wider context	
Taking practical steps to improve 8 Managing your inner performance 9 Navigating others' personality traits	

Where to next?

This chapter has outlined ways of negotiating around other people who have different personality traits from you. You have learned various methods for dealing with criticism, responding to a stimulus and managing rivalries and feuds, all of which may have been instigated by people who are viewing the world through a different set of filters from you.

In the next chapter you'll learn how to develop techniques for monitoring progress, which is a critical step in setting and achieving goals. Many people spend little time on this activity and, as a result, lose motivation and focus because they are not receiving information about what they have achieved.

10 Tracking and tuning performance

▶ *How should I monitor progress towards my goals?*

▶ *Measurement can be time consuming. How can I save time?*

▶ *Am I measuring the right things?*

▶ *I like taking action but not recording my results. How can I get round this?*

When you are working towards your overall objectives, it's important to measure your progress, for several reasons. First, you need to see whether you are proceeding in your desired direction so that you can decide what you need to adjust or change. Measuring progress helps you review what works, what doesn't work, and what actions are effective and making an impact.

As discussed in Chapter 5, people who write down their goals and then send weekly progress reports to their friends often accomplish significantly more than those who just write down their goals. This process is a form of tracking and tuning performance. This chapter will cover the three-step cycle of tracking, reflecting and tuning performance that will help you achieve sustainable change.

'Before you try to change something, increase your awareness of it.'

W. Timothy Gallwey, personal development coach (b. 1938)

→ The three-step performance cycle

The three main elements of monitoring performance – tracking, reflecting and tuning – need to be considered in relation to the process of how you work towards the results you want. It is also vital to consider how your behaviour is seen by other people who may be stakeholders in your success. The following diagram describes these three elements as a continuous cycle.

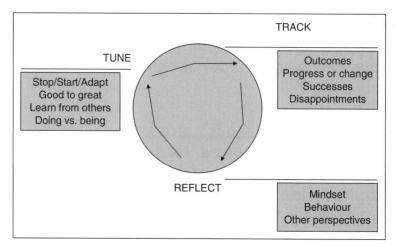

The three-step monitoring process

Tracking is the process of monitoring the outcomes you are aiming to achieve, and identifying whether there is progress or change. It is important to consider successes as well as disappointments in an objective manner.

Reflecting is the internal process of thinking seriously about what has happened, which can be in terms of both how you behaved and what you were thinking, as well as taking account of perspectives from others.

Tuning is the process by which you decide what you are going to change in order to get closer to your goal. It can be your mindset or it could be an activity.

Case study

A team of explorers was skiing to the North Pole. As there were no significant landmarks to aim for, it was hard for team members to know how far they had skied every day unless they used a system for measuring distance such as a GPS (global positioning system) to record their location using satellites. That data kept them motivated to some degree as they found out every evening what distance they had covered. However, the following morning, the measurement would demotivate them when they found out that their camp on the sea ice had floated backwards overnight, sometimes up to 4 kilometres (2.5 miles). This meant they had to cover some of the same ground again that day.

Their process for tracking, reflecting and tuning performance was:

▶ tracking – measuring the distance travelled and their current location using GPS

▶ reflecting – identifying the distance still to cover versus the amount of food left, and what that meant for them

▶ tuning – making the decision to walk farther each day to make up the shortfall.

→ Stakeholders

Value is in the eye of the stakeholder. Think about who has an involvement with, or a need to be kept informed of, your progress. These days, managers in organizations often begin a leadership development programme by completing a 360-degree assessment, where their manager, peers, team and external stakeholders are asked to evaluate certain competences (not traits) of that individual, which could be knowledge, skills or behaviours. Then the person identifies improvement areas and starts to work on changing their behaviour. After a period of months the same 360° process is carried out, which ideally indicates any improvements observed by their colleagues, managers, etc.

Marshall Goldsmith, in his book *What Got You Here Won't Get You There* (2008), describes a simple tracking and tuning process he calls 'Feedforward', which people can use with their colleagues on a regular basis. Goldsmith's research has shown that if individuals follow this process, there can be an improvement of up to 95 per cent in perceived leadership effectiveness.

Exercise 10.1

MARSHALL GOLDSMITH'S FEEDFORWARD PROCESS

1 Involve key stakeholders.

Ask several people whose feedback you value to help you in the following ways:

a Focus on the future and not on the past

b Encourage and support you

c Be honest

d Invite them to choose something to improve too, so they are part of the process and not judging you

2 Determine key behaviours for change.

Select up to three key areas for change that you are motivated to do something about.

a _____

b _____

c _____

3 Develop your action plan.

4 Ask your stakeholders on a regular basis for suggestions on how you can improve on the behaviours you wish to change.

These conversations are positive, simple and focused. They typically take 5–10 minutes and should ideally take place monthly.

How to have the conversation

▶ Be prepared; develop a 'script' that will guide the discussion, e.g. 'I am working on ... Can you give me one or two suggestions that might help me develop in this area?'

▶ Choose a setting where others will feel relaxed and comfortable when providing feedback.

▶ Thank the person for participating and giving you suggestions.

▶ Ask them to share what they want to improve, and then offer them one or two suggestions.

▶ Neither party needs to make any commitment; just ask for their ideas, listen and thank them.

▶ From all the ideas, there are likely to be two or three suggestions you'd like to take forward. Focus on these.

▶ Develop an ongoing follow-up process.

Go back monthly to find out what changes your stakeholders have noticed and what further suggestions they have.

5 Review what works and start again.

Stakeholders almost invariably report improvement because they have been actively involved in supporting your progress, and therefore are also alert to noticing that you are working on particular area.

....

→ Tracking

The tracking method you decide to use can affect your ability to achieve your outcome. If you track the wrong things, it can be demotivating, take you off course or be impossible to achieve. For example, if you wanted to win a gold medal at the Olympics and used that as the measure of your success, it would be difficult to achieve because you can control your own performance but you can't control the performance of your competitors.

However, if you change the method of tracking to a different measure, e.g. from an outcome-focused measure to a performance-focused one, perhaps aiming to improve your personal best time, then it brings the measure more into your control.

Exercise 10.2

MEASURES USED FOR TRACKING PROGRESS

The following table lists five goals and methods of tracking them. Decide whether you think the methods would be effective in helping a person towards their goal, and then list an alternative method for each goal.

When reviewing the methods of tracking, ask yourself the following questions.

▶ Is the measure within the control of the person setting the goal?

▶ Does it directly relate to what they want to achieve?

▶ Will the information help me learn about what to change or adapt?

Goal	Method of tracking	Effective? Yes/no	Your suggestion
To improve the relationship with my manager by listening more effectively.	My manager does not have to brief me more than once about each project		
To learn how to paint by joining the local art class and attending every week	Amount of money spent on art every week		
To lose 10 pounds in weight over the next three months	I will fit into my favourite summer dress which is now one size too small		
To be more organized at home so that I can invite my friends round to dinner and not be embarrassed	Number of meals I have organized this month		
To create a more structured approach to my day so that I can get more done	Did I get to the gym today?		

If you have a high score in conscientiousness, you are likely to enjoy tracking progress and may find it easy, as you tend to have the ability to work in a structured manner. However, be aware of the danger of focusing too much on doing the measuring rather than on what the information is telling you as a result. Remember the Pareto Principle (80:20 rule) and focus on tracking the things that really matter and are most likely to help you. It's easy to get caught up in focusing on small details or on something likely to be irrelevant.

TYPES OF MEASURE

You can use broadly two types of measure to track performance: quantitative and qualitative.

Quantitative measures refer to those outcomes that carry a numerical measure and show an observable change in behaviour. These outcomes are represented by increases, decreases, percentages and numbers. It is good to give the figure an indication of the period of time involved and a background statement which provides the contextual information. These types of measure require a baseline measurement in order to identify the differences that have occurred. An example is to increase sales in the next 12 months by 10 per cent based on last year's figures (£100,000 up to £110,000).

Qualitative measures refer to changes in learning, attitudes or experiences. Qualitative evidence tells us about changes that have taken place that individuals can see, feel or have responded to in some way. Measurement types include speaking to your colleagues, observation by yourself or others, or keeping a journal. An example is now feeling more confident to set an achievable goal than you did before you read this book.

Remember that people with different personality traits from you may prefer different methods, as the following table shows.

Personality dimension	High/low score	Preferred tracking method
Extraversion	Hi	May use a measure that can be talked through with someone else
	Lo	May want to keep the measure fairly private
Neuroticism	Hi	Make sure balanced measures as may focus on negative
	Lo	Ask for feedback from others to gain perspective
Conscientiousness	Hi	Help them focus on the most important measures and not get overwhelmed
	Lo	Prefer fewer details or structure, so create a simple measure
Agreeableness	Hi	Involve other people as part of the measurement process
	Lo	Make it practical
Openness to experience	Hi	Find a creative way of measuring
	Lo	Likely to prefer tried and tested ways of measuring

One example of a tracking method is that used in one organization where, at the end of a presentation delivered by an outside speaker, each member of the audience put a plastic coin in one of two bins labelled 'really enjoyable' and 'not great'. This provided the speaker with instant feedback. This idea might appeal to someone who has a high score on openness to experience and likes creative ways to measure things.

Alternatively, a person who has a low score on openness to experience may prefer a more conventional tracking method such as a chart like this one.

Indicator	Target	Quarter 1 result	Performance
Number of sales	327	332	Green
Customer service level	100%	83%	Amber
Profit	£4,000	£2,000	Red

Whatever form of measure you decide to go for, make sure that you are motivated to use it and to keep using it, because it is really only over time that you will be able to collect evidence of change.

→ Reflecting

The reflecting phase is when you use the data you have collected in order to think seriously about what it is telling you. Again, your personality traits will impact on how easy it is for you to reflect: some people may find they prefer to move straight to tuning, with little reflection after the tracking phase.

If you have a low score for extraversion, you are likely to enjoy the inner world of your thoughts and find being able to reflect easy. However, if this is combined with a high score on neuroticism, where you may be overly concerned about issues that appear less significant to others, indecisiveness may be a problem. This is likely if the outcomes being measured require some type of decision to be made, such as what to do differently.

This thinking process may be enhanced by getting the perspectives of others. Your confidant or buddy who is supporting you could provide valuable insight, particularly if you are prone to viewing the world in terms of 'a glass half empty'. Their feedback and questions may help you gain a more balanced perspective.

There are a number of methods that one can use to reflect on both mindset and behaviour. If you have not already done so, use the table at the end of each chapter to write down your observations and reflections. Taking a moment to complete those now will help you consider what you have learned so far.

Exercise 10.3

Look back at the four areas from Exercise 1.6, where you identified:

▶ where you take your energy (stimulus) from
▶ what you prefer to put your energies into.

This will help you identify different methods of reflection depending on each individual's preference. Think about what your preference is and tick the box below that is most like you.

External	People
Likely to enjoy talking experiences through with other people	*Will seek input from friends or confidant to get different perspective; likely to have more emotional content*
Internal	**Task**
May write diary, journal, spend time alone	*Focused on measures, facts, figures and analysis*

Exercise 10.4

GIBBS' MODEL OF REFLECTION

Gibbs' model of reflection (1988) below is a useful series of questions that you can use to take a structured approach to the entire learning cycle and develop some tuning actions for future progress.

Reflect on a situation or goal you have been working on already. Write your answers to the questions below or discuss your responses with a friend.

▶ Description

What happened? Don't make judgements yet or try to draw conclusions; simply describe.

_____

_____

▶ Feelings

What were your reactions and feelings? Again, don't move on to analysing these yet.

_____

_____

▶ Evaluation

What was good or bad about the experience? Make value judgements.

_____

_____

▶ Analysis

What sense can you make of the situation? What was really going on?

_____

_____

Were different people's experiences similar or different in important ways?

_____

_____

▶ Conclusions (general)

What can be concluded, in a general sense, from these experiences and the analyses you have undertaken?

_____

_____

▶ Conclusions (specific)

What can be concluded about your own specific, unique, personal situation or way of working?

_____

_____

▶ Personal action plans

What are you going to do differently in this type of situation next time? What steps are you going to take on the basis of what you have learned?

_____

_____

→ Tuning

The tuning process is when you take the information from the tracking element, combine it with your reflections and make some decisions about what to change, if anything. You may decide on some things to stop, start or adapt. Motivation is another variable at this time. If the feedback you receive, combined with your reflections, leads you to believe that it's too difficult to keep going, or that it will cause you to have to adapt your personality in a way that you would prefer not to, you may decide to give up.

It is worth reiterating at this stage the three elements of goal orientation described in Chapter 5, because they can have an impact on behaviour at this tuning stage. The three elements are:

1 **mastery goal** orientation – where the focus in on learning and improving ability

2 **performance approach** orientation – where the focus is on demonstrating competence

3 **performance avoidance** orientation – trying to avoid revealing lack of competence.

For example, say you want to be viewed by others as more engaging and you try out some new behaviours at an event. Then your confidant tells you that, while you did well, other people are still describing you as quiet. It may be your considered judgement that it's too difficult to change and you will only continue to show your lack of competence if you carry on.

It is vital that you try to keep going rather than think, 'I knew it would not work.' Your action instead may be to observe how others do it well, in order to try something different next time and also to pay attention to how you are thinking when you make the initial decision. (Exercise 8.5 on attributional thinking can help with this.)

Exercise 10.5

YOUR PROGRESS RECORD

Complete the progress record below to summarize the stage you have got to so far with your goal, as stated in the Introduction to the workbook.

My goal			My promise to myself	
My mantra			Supporter/confidant	
My expectations	Mindset	Tracking measures	My reflections	Tuning activities Stop–start–adapt Learn from others Be or do

If you are pleased with your progress and want to 'up your game', you can build on what you have achieved in several ways. Jim Collins, author of *Good to Great* (2001), offers some insights into what enables this to happen. He talks about four stages. First you need disciplined people, then disciplined thought, then disciplined action, and finally building greatness to last. The first three of his points have been covered in the chapters of this book so far, and his final point will be addressed in the next and final chapter.

Exercise 10.6

To review your journey from good to great, answer the questions below:

→ In what ways are you disciplined?

_____

_____

→ How can you learn from that and apply those principles in other parts of your life?

_____

_____

→ How comfortable are you to listen and accept the 'brutal facts', as Jim Collins describes them? What could you do in order to become more accepting of yourself and what needs to change? How can you build momentum to make changes and continue to keep doing so?

_____

_____

→ How can you create mechanisms that will enable you to sustain change into the future?

_____

_____

Your responses will help you take the final step of this workbook, in the final chapter.

What I have learned

REFLECTIONS

What are my thoughts, feelings and insights on what I have read so far?

YOUR JOURNEY

Summarize any actions you have identified as a result of reading this chapter.

Chapter	Actions
Introduction	
What is personality? 1 Personality: how temperament and character define you 2 Personality assessment tools and tests 3 How to use personality assessments	
What is personality? 4 The five dimensions of personality 5 Your personality, goal setting and achievement	
Setting goals 6 How to set goals that will motivate you 7 Positioning your goals in a wider context	
Taking practical steps to improve 8 Managing your inner performance 9 Navigating others' personality traits	
Monitoring progress 10 Tracking and tuning performance	

Where to next?

This chapter has outlined how you track and tune your performance in order to maintain progress and monitor motivation. The next chapter, on personality and persistence, will help you learn how to build resilience and mental toughness. It summarizes and builds on the learning from the rest of the book and provides an opportunity for you to consider how you can continue to optimize your personality and maintain a healthy level of self-improvement.

11 Personality and persistence

> ► When I'm stressed I find it hard to keep focused on my goal. What can I do to keep going?
> ► How can I get my behaviour back to normal if I get stressed?
> ► What can I do to develop greater mental toughness?
> ► How can I maintain energy and enthusiasm for my goal?

One of the most difficult situations to cope with is when you become stressed or things get difficult and you have to dig deep to keep working towards your goal. Yet it is worth it to find a way to accomplish things you perhaps did not imagine were possible. In the previous chapter, you learned that certain measures can provide valuable information as well as keep you motivated on your journey towards your goals.

This chapter focuses on the characteristics of your personality that can help you recover from setbacks and keep you going when things get tough. These are resilience, understanding the shadow side of our personality, developing mental toughness and overcoming resistance.

'Energy and persistence conquer all things.'

Benjamin Franklin, politician (1706–90)

→ Resilience

The term resilience refers to our ability to cope with adversity and stress, something that many people face these days at work. A resilient person has a sense of confidence in their abilities, tends to view challenges as an opportunity rather than a problem, and has an ability to retain emotional control and commitment to a task despite setbacks.

Exercise 11.1

RESILIENCE AT WORK

Read the case study opposite and answer the questions below.

→ What aspects of his personality helped George to be resilient?

_____

→ What external factors influenced George's ability to achieve his goal?

_____

→ How would you describe George's level of confidence?

_____

→ How would you describe his level of commitment?

_____

George had a great track record in sales as well as a friendly and outgoing personality. Because he was so good at converting prospects into revenue for his company, his manager decided to set George a much more challenging sales target for the following quarter – in a territory where previous sales reps had had limited success. His manager did not expect George to achieve much: many competitors were willing to cut their prices in order to get the business and some of them had rather questionable ethics, so it was a tough job.

In the first month, George, buoyed by his previous successes, went out to meet potential customers with a high level of confidence. However, he soon ran into difficulties because the system used to log prospects crashed and he lost all the data. Then he went down with flu and was off work for a couple of weeks. On his return, he realized that he would have to work twice as hard to get anywhere near his sales target. With his earnings coming mostly from sales commission (i.e. his monthly basic salary was low), he needed to get new business and grow it rapidly if he was to achieve the earnings he had had in his previous role. The odds seemed to be stacked against him.

But George did not give up. Every day he started out with a positive mindset and a smile on his face. He was able to build rapport with people quickly and remember little details about each person he met, which meant that, despite having lost the database, he could still recall something that would make them feel that he really cared about getting their business. He continued to believe he would be successful. At the end of the quarter, despite the setbacks, George had achieved a good result, without resorting to questionable ethics or fiddling the figures. His determination to keep going had eventually paid off.

→ How would you describe his level of emotional control?

_____

→ What caused them to be like that?

_____

→ How do think George viewed challenges – as problems or opportunities?

_____

→ What can you learn from this case study that you can apply to your own situation?

_____

....

→ The shadow side of our personality

Most of the time, as we go about our lives, we operate in a positive manner that is in sync with the aspects of our personality that we generally display. However, at the times when we feel stressed or challenged we may show the 'shadow side' of our personality. This represents the part of us that we don't acknowledge.

The shadow is the part of us that we choose not to see and that may be of a vulgar or unacceptable nature. As is it not integrated or even acknowledged by our conscious mind, the shadow sits and waits in the unconscious, ready to burst out at inappropriate moments. However, according to William Miller (1991), we can choose to pay more attention to our shadow, by:

▶ asking for feedback from others

▶ becoming aware of our own projections

- ▶ paying attention to our own 'slips of tongue'
- ▶ paying attention to what we find humorous
- ▶ studying dreams, daydreams and fantasies.

When the shadow side of our personality appears, we may behave in a way that is unexpected and usually not helpful for achieving our goals. For example, one of the facets of extraversion is charisma. When individuals display charisma, they are attractive and compelling to be around. If their shadow side appears, however, this can turn into manipulation, which is unlikely to have positive consequences, at least for the person being manipulated.

Another example is an individual who has a high score for agreeableness and enjoys working in a co-operative and open atmosphere. They may find themselves getting stressed when they have to deal with controlling or demanding people and, as a result, overreact to any slight criticism and begin to question their own level of competence. This in turn generates a loss of confidence, where they are unable to view situations with the objectiveness that they had previously.

The way out of this self-defeating loop is to be proactive and take time for fun and engage in relaxing activities, or to talk to close friends who can validate your feelings. As a result of being proactive, you can reaffirm your competence, acknowledge your confidence and return to a better equilibrium.

Some of the personality assessment methods and tools described in Chapter 2 recognize this 'shadow side' in various ways. For example, the Birkman Method, which highlights 11 different behavioural components along with the type of behaviour that a person will usually display, also highlights underlying needs and the stress behaviours that may occur if those needs have not been met.

Similarly, with the Myer-Briggs Type Indicator, the shadow side is known as the 'inferior function' and is described as the out-of-character self we all experience at one time or another in response to stress. It's the area to which we give the smallest amount of conscious energy and the exact opposite of our normal 'dominant' function, therefore providing a type of balance for us as human beings.

Exercise 11.2

WHAT'S YOUR SHADOW BEHAVIOUR?

Use the table below to note down the shadow behaviour you would tend to display if you found yourself under stress in the situations described. Then fill in what you would do to return to a better sense of balance and equilibrium.

Preference	Possible stressors	Unhelpful 'shadow side' behaviour	What you would do to regain balance
Extraversion: interaction with the outside world of people and things	Adversarial attitudes; too much focus on data		
Introversion: interaction with the inner world of ideas	Too little time alone; being asked to 'wing it'		
People: energized by being sociable and enjoying being with others	Demanding people; too much focus on task; disregard of feelings		
Task: getting things done, organizing, solving problems	Disorganized environment; slow decision making		

It's likely that those around you will notice pretty quickly when you begin to display your shadow-side behaviour, because it's not what they are used to. As well as developing your own awareness of your shadow side, encourage your close friends and confidant to tell you what causes you to show your shadow side.

It's often a signal that your needs are not being met, and therefore the most important thing you can do is to be good to yourself and do something to meet those needs. It might mean spending time alone, finishing jobs one at a time rather than having a list of work in progress, seeking a calming atmosphere, talking to friends, having time to think, having a variety of tasks to focus on or being given freedom in action and thought, to name some examples.

The important thing is to be able to learn from your shadow side and not just keep repeating a similar pattern of behaviour without gaining new insight. Learn to adopt different behaviours when it does occur.

→ Mental toughness

Broadly, mental toughness, as defined by psychologist Peter Clough (2012), is a collection of attributes that determines in large part how people deal with challenges, stressors and pressure, irrespective of prevailing circumstances. Clough found mental toughness to be strongly correlated with performance, wellbeing (including perceived bullying), positive behaviours and aspiration.

In looking at how to measure and manage mental toughness, he identified the following four scales:

▶ **challenge:** how people respond to challenge and change

▶ **control:** the extent to which people believe they shape what happens around them

▶ **commitment:** how people respond to goals and targets

▶ **confidence:** how people respond to setbacks.

Within the control scale there are two subscales: emotional control and life control; and within the confidence scale there also two subscales: interpersonal confidence and confidence in abilities.

You can use these four components to help you reflect on your own mental toughness and understand better how you respond to stressors and pressures. They can also help you reflect on what might be the consequences of your behaviours and what might be effective activities for increasing your mental toughness.

Typically, people with low levels of mental toughness are more at risk of underachievement, while those with high levels of mental toughness will be personally effective but may well cause problems for those with whom they work. Whatever your current level of mental toughness, reflecting on situations of challenge, stress or pressure using the four components will give you valuable learning.

You can develop your mental toughness by going through a four-stage cycle of reflection:

1 **Diagnosis**

What caused the situation, what state were you and/or others in, and what were your and/or their reactions?

2 **Intervention**

What positive actions could you take and what else could you do to heighten your awareness and so avoid making an inappropriate response next time? What corrective actions or adjustments could you make?

3 **Evaluation**

What feedback could you obtain, and where and when is best for you to reflect? How can you test your reflections by checking that your thinking and/or assumptions are right?

4 **Retesting**

This is a very valuable part of the process for assessing the impact of directed intervention and feeds into the entire personal development cycle.

Exercise 11.3

HOW IS YOUR MENTAL TOUGHNESS?

On the following pages is a series of inventories, devised by Peter Clough and AQR, which cover the four components of mental toughness and their subscales. Against each inventory item, say how often you display each of these behaviours by ticking the appropriate box.

Challenge inventory	I do this...		
	all the time	sometimes	rarely
I like competition.			
I thrive in competitive situations because I like to be challenged.			
I will take the lead in the team because I enjoy the responsibility of the challenge.			
I will take part in a task even if I'm not very good at it.			
I ask questions so that I understand what's expected of me.			
I feel relaxed with major competitions and training exercises.			
I feel pressured to achieve a target.			
If I've failed at something before, I believe I'll be able to do it next time.			
I see competitions as an opportunity to 'show off'.			
I try to appear positive if I'm asked to do something I don't like or something new.			
I look for opportunities to be the best.			
I put myself forward for projects.			

Confidence in my abilities inventory	I do this...		
	all the time	sometimes	rarely
I like being the centre of attention.			
I like to ask questions and don't worry if it makes me look silly in front of others.			
I like taking risks because it means I'll probably make a mistake that I can learn from..			
I'm not scared of failure.			
I'm happy to have a go at most things.			
I enjoy 'showing off' my abilities in front of others.			
I do well at most things.			

Interpersonal confidence inventory	I do this...		
	all the time	sometimes	rarely
If someone has a different opinion from me, I enjoy trying to change their mind.			
When I'm in a discussion, I tend to be one of the most talkative, even if I don't know a lot about the topic.			
I deal well with assertive and competitive people.			
When I'm challenged by others, I tend to stand my ground.			
I don't worry about what other people think of me.			
I enjoy asking questions about lots of different things.			
I tend to influence others in my team quite easily.			

Commitment inventory	I do this...		
	all the time	sometimes	rarely
I like making promises and setting goals.			
Making promises and setting goals and targets excite me.			
I don't let myself get easily distracted.			
I don't get bored with a project or a piece of work.			
I don't pull attention away from a task to stop people from asking questions.			
I like competition and pressure.			
I like testing myself and proving to others that I can do something.			
I will work hard and out of work time to be the best I can be..			
I enjoy gaining further skills and knowledge because it's a way I can improve.			
I prioritize different tasks and projects so that I know what needs to be given more attention.			

Life control inventory	I do this...		
	all the time	sometimes	rarely
I like to work on more than one job at a time.			
I will have a go at most things because I believe I can learn something from them.			
I feel comfortable making decisions for myself or a group.			
I don't need supervision from other people.			
I am well organized. I arrive on time and have everything I need for a project.			
If a project or task gets difficult, I work hard to get through it.			
I feel I can make a difference by involving myself in a project or task.			
I am good at managing my time.			

Emotional control inventory	I do this...		
	all the time	sometimes	rarely
I don't show a reaction if other people criticize me.			
If a task doesn't go as planned, I stay calm and don't get annoyed at others in the team.			
I don't let my annoyance show if others 'have a go' at me.			
If I'm not performing as well as I should be at work, I don't get upset and let others see it.			

Review how many ticks you put in each column within each inventory. If there are far more ticks in 'all the time' than 'sometimes' or 'rarely', it means that you are average to high on that particular scale. If your results fall mostly in 'rarely' or 'sometimes', your score for that scale would be moderate to low.

▶ **What do the results tell you about your mental toughness?**

_____

▶ **Which component of mental toughness might you wish to focus on developing further?**

_____

··

→ # Identifying areas of resistance

One of the components of mental toughness, outlined earlier, is commitment. While you can be committed to achieving a goal, sometimes there will be situations when you find it hard to get started or move forwards. If that happens, the root cause of the resistance can often be found in one of three areas.

1 **Head.** Is the reason logical? There can be a rational or practical reason for resistance; for example, the airline you want to travel on does not operate on Sundays.

2 **Heart.** Is the reason to do with people or feelings? This is likely to involve an emotional aspect of dealing with others, for example when you want to avoid a difficult conversation.

3 **Guts.** Is it just a gut feeling? This is often an intuitive reason, or your sixth sense: it just doesn't feel right to take action at this time but you can't explain why.

By pinpointing the area of resistance and und...
whether it concerns an external factor (outs...
or an internal factor (your own head, heart...
find a way to move forwards.

OVERCOMING RESISTANCE

The following table lists some common statements that people make as their reasons for not progressing their goals. Alongside each statement is a question to help change the focus from what is stopping you to what could be done to move forward, with the built-in assumption that you can progress. When you are not making progress on your goal, the key is to ask yourself what type of obstacle it is and what you need to do in order to overcome it.

Resistance statement	Question/action to help you move forward
There are too many options to choose from, so I can't move forward.	What seems to be the most important option right now?
I've got distracted by something else.	What is the benefit of you taking another step towards the original goal?
I don't believe I can do it.	What do you need to help you believe it can be achieved?
There's not enough time.	How much time do you need to take just one small action?
I am waiting for someone else to take their action.	What can you do in the meantime?
Others say it's not worth while.	Do you believe it's worth while?
I need to have the plan written before I can do anything.	Is the first step then to write the plan? When will you do that?
It doesn't seem like 'me' to try this out.	Who would you have to be in order to take this action?
When the going gets tough, I give up.	What or who could help you to keep going?

HOW DOES YOUR PERSONALITY HELP OR HINDER YOUR PROGRESS?

Within the five dimensions of personality (see also Chapter 4) there are characteristic behaviours that can stop people progressing with their goals. Read those below and consider how your preferences help or hinder you.

Conscientiousness

A high score on this dimension means you tend to be well organized and to think carefully before acting. You are likely to have to-do lists and personal organizers. You may therefore be able to think ahead about all the likely issues that could cause a project or goal to be derailed before they ever happen. However, this may get in the way of you taking action.

→ How does your level of conscientiousness impact on your ability to make progress with your goals?

Agreeableness

People who are agreeable tend to be pleasant, friendly and accommodating in social situations. If you have a high level of this dimension, you are likely to be empathetic, considerate, generous and helpful. This may mean that you notice blockages that are emotional because you pay attention to these matters. However, you may tend to avoid situations requiring a level of conflict or challenge when dealing with others or taking any action that could cause you to be viewed in a negative light.

→ How does your level of agreeableness impact on your ability to make progress with your goals?

_____

Extraversion

If you have a high score for extraversion you are predominantly concerned with, and obtain satisfaction from, what is outside yourself. Therefore you may find it difficult to identify blockages that are within you, as you are more focused on the external world around you. If you are at the other end of the spectrum, you tend to be more internally aware and therefore likely to notice what's really stopping progress. Once you do, however, you may be reluctant to share this knowledge with others.

→ How does your level of extraversion impact on your ability to make progress with your goals?

_____

Neuroticism

The innate 'fight or flight' instinct that humans possess tends to be more highly tuned in those with a high level of neuroticism. If you have this greater sensitivity to spot potentially negative outcomes, you are likely to be able to identify the blockages in head, heart and guts that threaten progress towards goals. Your challenge is likely to be feeling safe enough to take action despite what you may view as potential obstacles.

→ How does your level of neuroticism impact on your ability to make progress with your goals?

_____

Openness

This trait involves active imagination, aesthetic sensitivity, attentiveness to inner feelings, preference for variety and curiosity. If you have a high score for openness, you will be able easily to connect to your sixth sense, or gut feeling. Your challenge can be to find a way to communicate in a meaningful way with others who are more logical or reasoned, because they are unlikely to accept 'I just sense it's not a good time to do this' as a valid reason not to progress on a project. This dimension tends to have a normal distribution curve; most people have a moderate score.

→ How does your level of openness impact on your ability to make progress with your goals?

_____

→ Review each of the five dimensions of personality as they relate to resistance and how you responded to each question. Note down which of the dimensions has the greatest impact on your ability to make progress with your goal.

_____

→ Now that you are aware of this, write down three ideas that you can put into practice, which will help you recognize and overcome this facet of your personality the next time it threatens to get in the way of what you want to achieve.

1 _____

2 _____

3 _____

Acknowledge the part of your personality that until now has had a positive intent to support you. Now accept that it no longer serves you in the way that you need it to, and that you will opt for one of the other ideas you came up with.

For example, a high level of agreeableness may mean that you avoid difficult conversations, which causes your plan to be delayed. One new idea is to prepare an outline of a conversation before you have it, and then look at the situation from the other person's perspective, to consider what would make it a productive conversation for them.

→ Write down your plan to overcome the less helpful dimension of your personality.

_____

_____

_____

What I have learned

REFLECTIONS

What are my thoughts, feelings and insights on what I have read so far?

```
┌─────────────────────────────────────┐
│                                     │
│                                     │
│                                     │
└─────────────────────────────────────┘
```

YOUR JOURNEY

Summarize any actions you have identified as a result of reading this chapter.

Chapter	Actions
Introduction	
What is personality? 1 Personality: how temperament and character define you 2 Personality assessment tools and tests 3 How to use personality assessments	
Assessing where you are 4 The five dimensions of personality 5 Your personality, goal setting and achievement	
Setting goals 6 How to set goals that will motivate you 7 Positioning your goals in a wider context	
Taking practical steps to improve 8 Managing your inner performance 9 Navigating others' personality traits	
Monitoring progress 10 Tracking and tuning performance 11 Personality and persistence	

Where to next?

This chapter has outlined different ways in which you can maintain motivation and resilience as you progress towards your goals. You have learned that these ways include understanding and dealing with the shadow side of your personality, increasing your mental toughness and overcoming your resistance. The next and final chapter will help you anticipate and prepare to apply the learning from this workbook when you are setting and achieving your future goals.

12

Get where you want to be: your future focus

- ▶ Knowing my personality, what can I do to anticipate how I may behave in future situations?
- ▶ How will I sustain the learning from this book in the future?
- ▶ How do I create a new habit?
- ▶ Which section of the book should I now pay most attention to?

By now you should be clearer about how your personality affects how you set and achieve goals as well as leading to the situations or behaviours that you want to change. It is important to reiterate the point made at the beginning of this book: it *is* possible to change aspects of your personality because personality is a combination of traits you are born with and habits you have developed over time.

This chapter will help you review what you have learned in this workbook and identify the areas that you want to focus on, in order to get different results. It will explore how to change behaviour, how to create new habits and how to sustain that change into the future.

> 'We continue to shape our personality all our life.
> If we knew ourselves perfectly, we should die.'
>
> Albert Camus, author and philosopher (1913–60)

Exercise 12.1

REVIEW THE JOURNEY

Over the previous 11 chapters you have undertaken a series of activities to help you understand more about how your personality affects how you set and achieve goals.

Revisit the original intention that you wrote down in Exercise A in the Introduction – what you would like to achieve as a result of reading this book.

Then review the learning/actions that you wrote down at the end of each chapter. Then write down which action or learning point:

1 – you are most open to trying out

2 – you need to put into practice

3 – might be the most difficult and yet most rewarding.

Chapter	Action	Does it take you towards your goal?
Introduction		
What is personality? (Chapters 1, 2 and 3)		
Assessing where you are now (Chapters 4 and 5)		
Setting goals (Chapters 6 and 7)		
Taking practical steps to improve (Chapters 8 and 9)		
Monitoring progress (Chapters 10 and 11)		
The future (Chapter 12)		

Now that you have identified actions that you wish to take, the challenge will be to try them out and sustain the behaviour change into the future. Think about how you normally approach carrying out an action. Do you leave it until the last minute? Do you try to ignore it? What would encourage you to change your behaviour?

....

→ Changing your behaviour

In order to change your behaviour, you have to unpick the process for doing this, as already outlined in part in Exercise 8.5. Begin with the situation you want to change. It may be how you react when you have to speak to someone you find frustrating, or it could be how to behave when you set a goal but don't follow through, or anything else that you want to change.

Situation ⟶ Thoughts ⟶ Feelings ⟶ Behaviour

Exercise 12.2

Using the prompts in the following table, analyse how the situation led to thoughts, which generated feelings that drove the behaviour.

Situation	Thoughts	Feelings	Behaviour
Write down what happened in that situation. Make sure you're objective in how you describe it.	What were your thoughts at that moment? You can analyse them into the categories below as: **Rational thoughts** · Is it a fact? · Are you sure of it? · Does it happen to everyone? · Does it happen in all situations? **Irrational thoughts** · Black and white thinking – always/never · Mind reading: 'I think no one will listen' · Using phrases like 'I should' · Overreacting or exaggerating · Thinking in disasters: 'It's going to be a nightmare' · Foretelling the future /digging up the past	What were your feelings? Think this through as carefully as you can, generally categorizing them into: - afraid - sad - angry - happy	What behaviour did that generate as a result?

Next, create a new goal by focusing on the behaviour you want first of all and then describing how you want to feel and how you want to think.

Behaviour	Feelings	Thoughts	Situation
Write down the new behaviour that you would like to have, e.g. 'I'd like to take charge and volunteer myself as leader in our group.' Be prepared to lower your standards so that you can aim for something that you think is achievable. Once that's done, you can then set the bar a little higher next time.	Identify how you will want to feel, e.g. confident, relaxed, happy.	Consider how you want to think about the situation, e.g. 'I can do a good job as leader just as well as anyone else in the group. It will be fun to give it a try.'	Now give it a try and see what happens, while being aware of your thinking. If things go awry, check that you are thinking rationally and not irrationally.

While you are trying this out, you will also have to recognize that you may be fighting against habits that you have developed over many years. Habits are our brain's way of streamlining our behaviour patterns to make us operate more efficiently and develop automatic behaviour in response to cues.

In his book *The Power of Habit* (2012), Charles Duhigg talks about the three phases in a habit: the cue, the routine and the reward. For example, every day at 10 a.m. (the cue) you switch the kettle on and make a cup of tea (routine) and enjoy it with a biscuit (the reward).

In order to change your habits, he argues, you must first identify the routine (what it is that you do that you want to change) before you can experiment with different rewards. Then you can isolate the cue, which generally can be categorized as one of the following: location, time, emotional state, other people or the immediately preceding action. Finally, you create a plan to change the habit. Duhigg advocated a four-step process for this, as shown in the next exercise.

Exercise 12.3

DUHIGG'S STEPS TO CHANGING A HABIT

Charles Duhigg developed a four-step process for changing a habit. In the following example, when someone asks a question (cue), you answer back without thinking (routine) because it makes you feel smart (reward). The process shows you how to plan for the cue and identify a different behaviour that will satisfy the reward you are craving.

Stage	Example
1 Identify the routine	Answering back without thinking
2 Experiment with rewards	Completing a crossword Asking a great question back Talking about a wide range of subjects
3 Isolate the cue	Ask yourself the following questions: • Where am I? • What time is it? • What is my emotional state? • Who else is here? • What action immediately precedes the urge?
4 Create a plan to change the habit	When someone asks me a question, I will demonstrate I am smart by asking them a great question back, which helps them clarify exactly what they want to know.

Now use the same format to change one of your habits, remembering that when you see 'cue', you will do a routine in order to get a reward.

Stage	Example
1 Identify the routine	
2 Experiment with rewards	
3 Isolate the cue	
4 Create a plan to change the habit	

→ Creating new neural pathways

By trying out new behaviours, you are encouraging your brain to develop new neural pathways rather than just using 'automatic pilot'. These new pathways are created by neurons which fire and get connected together over time.

Existing messages in our heads may feel as if they are facts but they are merely our learned experiences, often developed during childhood, which have formed strong neural pathways. These messages become the narrative of our lives, they tell us who (we think) we are, and they are accepted as reality.

However, this narrative can limit us, as this workbook has tried to show. It has been written as a way of helping you to understand how it is possible to change those neural pathways and adapt your personality. The techniques and exercises that you have worked through should help you respond better to situations rather than having a 'knee-jerk' reaction to stressful situations. It's about creating new habits that will deliver more effective behaviours for you.

Exercise 12.4

FUTURE PACING

As you plan how you are going to behave differently in future, and aim to develop this new behaviour into a habit, there is a technique you can use called 'future pacing'. It comes from the world of neuro-linguistic programming, and it can help you connect your changes to future situations, so that you are able to imagine your new behaviour at that time.

1 Identify the new habit or behaviour that you are going to have from now on.

_____

2 Think of four possible future situations that would have previously triggered the old behaviour that you don't want to have any more. Examples might be when you are challenged by a colleague or have to speak to a particular individual in your team.

▶ _____

▶ _____

▶ _____

▶ _____

3 Imagine the first situation with you behaving in your new way. Think about what you will now see, hear and feel at that time. Does the change hold? Do you respond in the way you would like?

_____

_____

_____

4 Consider whether you need to make further changes to fine-tune the desired response.

_____

5 Repeat steps 3 and 4 for the other three situations.

_____

_____

_____

What you are doing is preparing your unconscious mind to expect you to behave in the new way when there are no immediate pressures or threats. This helps again to reinforce new neural pathways.

....

→ Combinations of the five dimensions

In this workbook the Big Five dimensions of personality have been used as a thread running through each chapter to describe the five basic personality traits. You should by now have developed a clearer sense of the traits that serve you well, and those that get in the way of you achieving what you want to.

As you go forward from here, it may be worth considering how these traits combine, which will give a higher-level perspective on your personality. John Digman (1997) proposed categorizing the factors into two areas shown below, with Colin DeYoung and colleagues (2002) defining these categories into stability and plasticity. While this is not a unanimously accepted model, it seems that the focus on internal and external traits can be helpful for understanding their impact.

Alpha factors (stability)	Beta factors (plasticity)
Agreeableness Conscientiousness Neuroticism	Extraversion Openness to experience
These traits are about our ability to display a positive or negative expression of socially desirable traits – thus a focus towards community and being around others, our ability to maintain relationships, motivation and emotional states.	These traits are focused more inwardly and on our ability to strive for mastery, power and self-assertion. They are about our ability to reduce our inhibitions as well as display cognitive flexibility.

Exercise 12.5

Think about where you go next. What type of adaptations do you want to make to your personality in the future? Are they:

▶ external – related to your ability to maintain relationships, motivation or emotional state?

▶ internal – related to your ability to reduce your inhibitions or personal growth?

➜ Which trait(s) are likely to be related to the changes you want to make?

_____

_____

_____

➜ What have you learned by reading this book that will help you to change in the future?

_____

_____

_____

➜ Who can support you?

_____

➜ Note down what you are going to do, by when, and how you will know you have been successful.

_____

_____

_____

→ Sustaining change

You now have the tools, understanding and, it's hoped, the motivation to sustain any behaviour changes you make into the future. Here are some tips to help you.

▶ **Focus on the present**
It is far easier to be aware of your thoughts, feelings and behaviours in the 'now' than to imagine the future, so make small adjustments to what you are doing and how you are behaving today. Don't wait until tomorrow.

▶ **Commit time to translate the learning into habits**
Make sure you are realistic about what you can achieve, and commit enough time to take the action you need. Everyone can find ten minutes a day to do something different, so consider what is a realistic goal to achieve in the time you are willing to commit.

▶ **Develop the skill**
Make sure you know what you need to do, and if you have not found the answer in this book, find out how you can develop the skill you need.

▶ **Gauge your motivation**
Connect your change to your longer-term goals and aspirations – that way, you can see the reason why you should keep going with the change.

▶ **Create a routine**
Remember the routine element of the habit-forming process in Exercise 12.3. Create an easy way to make sure you take the action day after day, time after time.

▶ **Seek support**
It's hard to sustain change if you are the only one focusing on it. Find a confidant or buddy to help support you on the journey. If you both focus on something, it becomes a real peer-to-peer exercise.

Now imagine yourself six months from now. What will you have achieved? And what will that have enabled you to do or be that is different from today?

What I have learned

YOUR JOURNEY

Summarize any actions you have identified as a result of reading this chapter.

Chapter	Actions
Introduction	
What is personality? 1 Personality: how temperament and character define you 2 Personality assessment tools and tests 3 How to use personality assessments	
Assessing where you are 4 The five dimensions of personality 5 Your personality, goal setting and achievement	
Setting goals 6 How to set goals that will motivate you 7 Positioning your goals in a wider context	
Taking practical steps to improve 8 Managing your inner performance 9 Navigating others' personality traits	
Monitoring progress 10 Tracking and tuning performance 11 Personality and persistence	
The future 12 Get where you want to be: your future focus	

Final thought

As you will have learned in this book, your personality makes you unique and therefore different from everyone else. This is through the combination of innate traits you were born with and the habits you have developed over time.

Having worked through the exercises in this book, you will have gained insight into how your personality influences how you set and achieve goals, as well as the manner in which you do so. You will also have reflected on how to work with people who may be very different from you.

It is now your choice what you do with this knowledge. Use it to set yourself goals that you did not think were achievable, feel more confident to adapt your style around others, and commit to living a life that helps you be the best you possible.

Don't just dream it – do it now!

References

CHAPTER 2

For a fuller explanation of psychophysics, see Baird, J. C. and Noma, E., *Fundamentals of Scaling and Psychophysics*, p. 1 (Wiley series in behaviour, 1978).

For more information about the Myers-Briggs type indicator, see www.mbti.org

For more about Belbin team types, see www.belbin.com

The DiSC Model of Behaviour was first proposed by William Moulton Marston in his 1928 book *Emotions of Normal People* (Read Books, 2007).

For more information about Eysenck's work on the two personality dimensions of extraversion and neuroticism, see his *Dimensions of Personality* (original 1947).

CHAPTER 3

http://mbtitoday.org/wp-content/uploads/N-Quenk-on-Type-and-Trait.pdf

http://en.wikipedia.org/wiki/16PF_Questionnaire

CHAPTER 4

Andrew Costa and John M. McCrae's 1992 research is often recognized, although credit should be given to earlier models postulated by Ernest Tupes and Raymond Christal.

Nettle, D., *Personality* (Oxford: Oxford University Press, 2007)

McCrae, R. R. and Costa, P. T. Jr., *Personality in adulthood: A five-factor theory perspective,* 2nd ed. (New York: The Guilford Press. Florida: Psychological Assessment Resources, Inc., 2003)

Questionnaire courtesy of Quantum Corporate Coaching www.quantumdp.com

CHAPTER 5

Cooperrider, D. L. and Whitney, D., *Appreciative Inquiry: A Positive Revolution in Change* (San Francisco: Berrett-Koehler, 2005)

Hill, N., *Think and Grow Rich* (London: Vermilion, 2004)

Gail Matthews, PhD, Dominican University, *Summary of Recent Goals Research* (PDF here: Gail Matthews' *Written Goal Study,* Dominican University)

Darryl Stevens, http://singlecellrebel.blogspot.co.uk/

CHAPTER 6

Alamdari, F. and Fagan, S., 'Impact of the Adherence to the original low-cost model on the profitability of low-cost airlines', *Transport Reviews* 25(3), 377–90 (2005).

Dilts, R. B. and DeLozier, J. A., *Encyclopedia of Systemic Neuro-Linguistic Programming and NLP New Coding* (Scotts Valley: NLP University Press, 2000)

CHAPTER 7

Hollenbeck, J. R. and Klein, H. J., 'Goal commitment and the goal-setting process: Problems, prospects, and proposals for future research', *Journal of Applied Psychology,* 72, 212–20 (1987)

Stockdale, S. and Steeper, C., *Cope with Change at Work* (London: Hodder, 2012)

Nutley, T., 'Critical Success Factors Questionnaire' (UK College of Personal Development, adapted from Robert Dilts' work on Success Factor Modelling, 2006)

Seligman, M. E. P., *Helplessness: On Depression, Development, and Death* (San Francisco: W. H. Freeman, 1975)

Weiner, B., *An attributional theory of motivation and emotion* (New York: Springer-Verlag, 1986)

CHAPTER 8

Trickey, G. and Yeung, S. Y., *Managing Risk: The Human Factor* (Tunbridge Wells: PCL, November 2011)

For more information on the Risk-Type Compass see www.psychological-consultancy.com

Campbell, J. P., 'Modeling the performance prediction problem in industrial and organizational psychology', in M. D. Dunnette and L. M. Hough (eds.), *Handbook of industrial and organizational psychology,* pp. 687–732 (Palo Alto, CA: Consulting Psychologists Press, 1991)

CHAPTER 9

Criticalthinking.net

Ennis, R. H., *Twenty-One Strategies and Tactics for Teaching Critical Thinking* (rhennis@illinois.edu 2011)

CHAPTER 10

Goldsmith, M., *What Got You Here Won't Get You There: How successful people become even more successful* (London: Profile Books, 2008)

www.marshallgoldsmithlibrary.com

Gibbs, G., *Learning by doing: A guide to teaching and learning methods*, Oxford Centre for Staff and Learning Development (London: Further Education Unit, 1988)

Collins, J., *Good to Great* (New York: Harper Business, 2001)

CHAPTER 11

Miller, W. A., 'Finding the Shadow in Daily Life', in J. Abrams and C. Zweig (eds), *Meeting the Shadow: The Hidden Power of the Dark Side of Human Nature* (pp. 38–44) (New York: St Martin's Press, 1990)

This definition for mental toughness was developed by Clough and Strycharczyk (AQR). For more information, read Clough, P. and Strycharczyk, D., *Developing Mental Toughness* (London: Kogan Page, 2012)

Exercise 11.5: Acknowledgement to AQR Ltd for use of this exercise. AQR is a leading psychometric test publisher and business consultancy, offering a range of psychometric tests, tools and development programmes. For more information go to www.aqr.co.uk

CHAPTER 12

Exercise 12.3: Acknowledgement to Charles Duhigg for the use of this exercise. See also Duhigg, C., *The Power of Habit* (Toronto: Random House, 2012)

Digman, J. M. 'Higher-order factors of the Big Five', *Journal of Personality and Social Psychology*, 73(6), pp. 1246–56 (1997)

DeYoung, C. G., Peterson, J. B. and Higgins, D. M., 'Higher-order factors of the Big Five predict conformity: Are there neuroses of health?' *Personality and Individual Differences*, 33, 533–52 (2002)

Follow-up worksheets

Worksheet 1

REVERSE BRAINSTORMING NOTES

How can I

.... ?

Reverse statement is

....

....

....

Ideas	Ideas reversed
1	
2	
3	
4	
5	
6	
7	
8	

What have I learned as a result?

Worksheet 2

MY ACTION PLAN

What do I want to do differently as a result of reading this book?

1 _____

_____

_____

_____

_____

_____

2 _____

_____

_____

_____

_____

_____

_____

3 _____

_____

_____

_____

_____

_____

_____

4 _____

_____

_____

_____

_____

_____

5 _____

_____

_____

_____

_____

Worksheet 3

DIARY FOR WEEK 1

Note down your successes for each day.

Sunday	
Monday	
Tuesday	
Wednesday	
Thursday	
Friday	
Saturday	

REFLECTIONS ON WEEK 1

What did I want to achieve this week?	
What happened, and why in that way?	
How did I think, feel and respond?	
So what is the learning for me?	
What will I do differently next week?	

Worksheet 4

DIARY FOR WEEK 2

Note down your successes for each day.

Sunday	
Monday	
Tuesday	
Wednesday	
Thursday	
Friday	
Saturday	

REFLECTIONS ON WEEK 2

What did I want to achieve this week?	
What happened, and why in that way?	
How did I think, feel and respond?	
So what is the learning for me?	
What will I do differently next week?	

Worksheet 5

DIARY FOR WEEK 3

Note down your successes for each day.

Sunday	
Monday	
Tuesday	
Wednesday	
Thursday	
Friday	
Saturday	

REFLECTIONS ON WEEK 3

What did I want to achieve this week?	
What happened, and why in that way?	
How did I think, feel and respond?	
So what is the learning for me?	
What will I do differently next week?	

Worksheet 6

DIARY FOR WEEK 4

Note down your successes for each day.

Week 3

Sunday	
Monday	
Tuesday	
Wednesday	
Thursday	
Friday	
Saturday	

REFLECTIONS ON WEEK 4

What did I want to achieve this week?	
What happened, and why in that way?	
How did I think, feel and respond?	
So what is the learning for me?	
What will I do differently next week?	

What next?

Having taken action and reflected on learning over the last month, to what degree have I moved further towards my goals?

What will I do to sustain my learning in the future?

Index

The PERSONALITY Workbook

Sue Stockdale and Clive Steeper